The Complete Guide to
UNDERSTANDING
AND USING

NLP

DISCARD

NEURO-LINGUISTIC
PROGRAMMING
EXPLAINED SIMPLY

Barbara P. Gibson

THE COMPLETE GUIDE TO UNDERSTANDING AND USING NLP: NEURO-LINGUISTIC PROGRAMMING EXPLAINED SIMPLY

Copyright © 2011 Atlantic Publishing Group, Inc.
1405 SW 6th Avenue • Ocala, Florida 34471 • Phone 800-814-1132 • Fax 352-622-1875
Web site: www.atlantic-pub.com • E-mail: sales@atlantic-pub.com
SAN Number: 268-1250

Library of Congress Cataloging-in-Publication Data

Gibson, Barbara Patrice, 1966-
 The complete guide to understanding and using NLP : neuro-linguistic programming explained simply / by Barbara P. Gibson.
   p. cm.
 Includes bibliographical references and index.
 ISBN-13: 978-1-60138-382-2 (alk. paper)
 ISBN-10: 1-60138-382-7 (alk. paper)
 1. Neurolinguistic programming. I. Title.
 BF637.N46G53 2010
 158.1--dc22

                                 2010045756

Printed in the United States

Printed on Recycled Paper

PROJECT MANAGER: Melissa Peterson • mpeterson@atlantic-pub.com
INTERIOR LAYOUT: Antoinette D'Amore • addesign@videotron.ca
PROOFREADER: Brett Daly • brett.daly1@gmail.com
FRONT/BACK COVER DESIGNS: Jackie Miller • millerjackiej@gmail.com

We recently lost our beloved pet "Bear," who was not only our best and dearest friend but also the "Vice President of Sunshine" here at Atlantic Publishing. He did not receive a salary but worked tirelessly 24 hours a day to please his parents. Bear was a rescue dog that turned around and showered myself, my wife, Sherri, his grandparents Jean, Bob, and Nancy, and every person and animal he met (maybe not rabbits) with friendship and love. He made a lot of people smile every day.

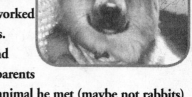

We wanted you to know that a portion of the profits of this book will be donated to The Humane Society of the United States. *–Douglas & Sherri Brown*

The human-animal bond is as old as human history. We cherish our animal companions for their unconditional affection and acceptance. We feel a thrill when we glimpse wild creatures in their natural habitat or in our own backyard.

Unfortunately, the human-animal bond has at times been weakened. Humans have exploited some animal species to the point of extinction.

The Humane Society of the United States makes a difference in the lives of animals here at home and worldwide. The HSUS is dedicated to creating a world where our relationship with animals is guided by compassion. We seek a truly humane society in which animals are respected for their intrinsic value, and where the human-animal bond is strong.

Want to help animals? We have plenty of suggestions. Adopt a pet from a local shelter, join The Humane Society and be a part of our work to help companion animals and wildlife. You will be funding our educational, legislative, investigative and outreach projects in the U.S. and across the globe.

Or perhaps you'd like to make a memorial donation in honor of a pet, friend or relative? You can through our Kindred Spirits program. And if you'd like to contribute in a more structured way, our Planned Giving Office has suggestions about estate planning, annuities, and even gifts of stock that avoid capital gains taxes.

Maybe you have land that you would like to preserve as a lasting habitat for wildlife. Our Wildlife Land Trust can help you. Perhaps the land you want to share is a backyard—that's enough. Our Urban Wildlife Sanctuary Program will show you how to create a habitat for your wild neighbors.

So you see, it's easy to help animals. And The HSUS is here to help.

THE HUMANE SOCIETY
OF THE UNITED STATES.

2100 L Street NW • Washington, DC 20037 • 202-452-1100
www.hsus.org

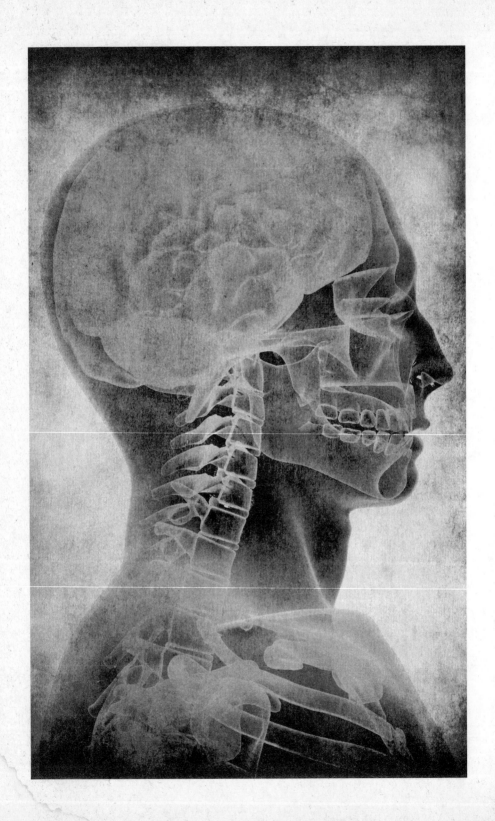

Dedication

For Zachary

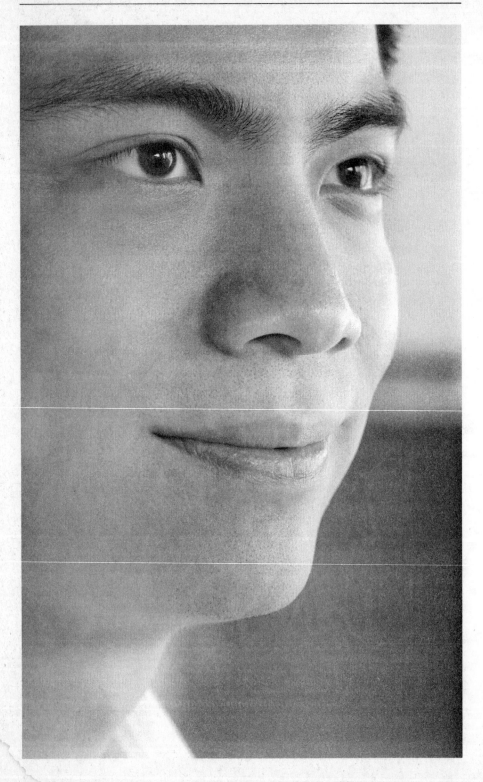

Table Of Contents

Introduction **15**

Chapter 1: What is Neuro-linguistic Programming? **27**

The Four Learning Levels of NLP 28

    Subconscious incompetence 28

    Conscious incompetence 28

    Conscious competence 29

    Subconscious competence 29

History of NLP 30

Presuppositions of NLP 34

    The map is not the territory 34

    People respond based on their individual map 36

    There is no failure — only feedback 37

*The meaning of communication
is the response it gets*.. 40

*If what you are doing is not working,
do something different*.. 41

You cannot not communicate... 42

*Individuals have all the resources
they need to achieve their desired outcomes*................. 43

Underlying every behavior is a positive intent.............. 44

People are much more than their behavior.................... 45

People make the best choices available to them........... 45

*Modeling successful performance
leads to excellence*... 48

The Growth of NLP... 48

Criticism of NLP... 49

Case Study: Successful Use of NLP 51

Chapter 2: What Can You Do with NLP? 55

What Do You Want NLP to Do for You?............................ 58

Using dissociation to eliminate fear............................... 62

Eye movement desensitization and reprocessing.......... 64

Reprocessing 64

The Value of NLP in Professional Settings....................... 68

NLP for business communication.................................... 73

NLP is a technique for influencing others 75

Create strong partnerships with NLP 75

Increase productivity with NLP....................................... 76

Use NLP to Align Values Around Success 77

Improve negotiation skills with NLP 78

Tools for Creating Rapport 82

Matching 82

Mirroring 82

Pacing for Rapport 83

How else can NLP help you at work? 87

The Value of NLP in Education 89

*Use NLP to improve the educational
experience for teachers and students............................ 90*

Promote positive learning behaviors 93

Six NLP strategies for the teacher's tool box................. 94

Robert Dilts on creating change................................... 105

Use NLP in Your Personal Life 108

The Value of NLP in improving relationships 109

Release phobias and painful memories........................ 109

Decrease stress and anxiety 110

Eliminate unwanted behaviors.................................... 111

How to design a well-formed goal 113

Take action 116

Perceptual positions.. 117

Use NLP to improve self-image 120

The Circle of Excellence pattern.................................. 121

Case Study: The Benefits of NLP 123

Chapter 3: The Pillars of NLP 129

Behavioral Flexibility 129

Sensory Acuity.. 130

Rapport 131

Outcome Thinking.. 134

Chapter 4: Focus on the Outcome Frame ...137

Outcome Frame Defined 138

*Five conditions for transforming goals
into outcomes*.. *138*

Internal resources for achieving outcomes *144*

*Material or external resources
for achieving outcomes* *145*

Case Study: Life Transformations with NLP 147

Chapter 5: Understanding
Communication.. 153

How Do We Communicate? 154

Predicates.. *156*

How can predicates improve communication?............. *156*

Eye-accessing cues... *157*

Case Study: The Benefits of NLP 161

Chapter 6: Metaprograms 165

Mental Processes 166

Filters that Determine How the World is Viewed............ 167

   Working with limiting beliefs *167*

Common Factors in Resistance to Change 168

How to Use Metaprograms in NLP.............................. 169

   Common metaprograms... *170*

Identifying Metaprograms 173

Case Study: Helping Clients Change
Behaviors and Develop New Skills with NLP................. 177

Chapter 7: Anchoring.................................. 181

Anchors and Future Pacing 181

   Positive anchors.. *182*

   Negative anchors *184*

   External stimuli that evoke an internal response *186*

   *Link a positive state to a past occasion
   and relive it to set it* *187*

Creating Positive Anchors 190

   *Resource — an anchor that genuinely
   provides good feelings* *194*

   *Collapsing — a process for breaking
   negative anchors* *194*

Using Anchors Effectively 197

   *Eliciting and calibrating — evoking a feeling and
   identifying the associated behavior and language*...... *200*

   Using the TOTE model to check your progress *201*

   Altering states with anchors...................................... *202*

Chapter 8: Submodalities 205

Fine Tuning Modalities (Representational Systems) 205

Finer distinctions of senses
(visual, auditory, kinesthetic) 206

Visual submodalities may include
brightness or color 210

Auditory submodalities may include
pitch or volume 211

Kinesthetic submodalities may include
texture or emotion 212

Using the Swish Pattern to Make Behavioral Changes ... 213

Rapid submodality shifts associate
two mental images 215

Case Study: Jonathan Royle on the Magic of NLP 224

Chapter 9: The Meta and Milton Models ... 229

Meta Model Processes 230

Distortions 230

Generalizations... 231

Deletions 232

Using the Meta Model 234

The Milton Model.. 243

Milton model language patterns 244

Uses of the Milton model... 245

Chapter 10: NLP Patterns 247

Patterns are Directions for
Creating Effective Experiences 247

Presentation of Several Basic Patterns 248

The Autobiography pattern.. 248

Additional Patterns 250

The Phobia Cure pattern.. 250

The As-if pattern 251

The Forgiveness pattern 252

Visual Squash pattern 253

Conclusion.. 257

NLP in Sales 258

Transforming goals into well-formed outcomes 259

NLP for Successful Communication 260

Behavioral flexibility 261

Sensory acuity... 261

Rapport... 261

Outcome thinking... 261

NLP in Education.. 262

Six NLP strategies for the teacher's tool box............... 262

NLP for Personal Change 263

NLP for Understanding Motivation 264

Presuppositions 266

The map is not the territory 266

People respond based on their individual map 266

There is no failure — only feedback 266

*The meaning of communication
is the response it gets* 267

*If what you are doing is not working,
do something different* 267

You cannot not communicate 268

*Individuals have all the resources they need
to achieve their desired outcomes* 268

Underlying every behavior is a positive intent 269

People are much more than their behavior 270

People make the best choices available to them 270

*NLP is growing in popularity
in motivational circles* 271

*Use the techniques to improve
both professional and personal lives* 272

References for Further Study 273

Glossary **275**

Bibliography **281**

Author Biography **283**

Index **285**

Introduction

Many people have felt stuck in patterns that kept them from realizing their goals, or they cannot change habits they know hold them back. Neurolinguistic programming (NLP) offers a way to create new patterns and achieve excellence in virtually every area of your life. This book presents a basic overview of NLP, outlines some of its benefits, and provides strategies for using NLP to achieve your goals.

NLP is about how you take in information through your senses and decide what it means or represent it in your mind. Perhaps you feel skeptical about the benefits of learning about and practicing NLP. That is good. NLP is not a magic wand or cure all; it is a tool. You will only achieve success with NLP if you choose to apply the tools. No special tricks, degrees, or gimmicks are required to achieve success with NLP. Admittedly, it will take practice. As you become more comfortable with the ideas and exercises, you will learn more about yourself and others. You will also feel empowered by your ability to create the changes you want in your life. A basic premise of NLP is if anything can be accomplished, that same thing can be accomplished again. NLP will show you how to accomplish goals, such as meeting a sales goal, changing unhealthy eating habits, or improving a relationship. NLP combines three distinct components. *Neuro* relates to the brain and the neurological processes involved with sending and receiving information; *linguistic* concerns the verbal and nonverbal information the brain processes; and finally, *programming* relates to how verbal and nonverbal information sent and received by the brain is interpreted or assigned meaning. In other words, NLP is a fancy name for a combination of processes you do all the time without much thought, such as thinking, seeing, and deciding. NLP gives you the tools to direct these processes in a way that supports your desired outcomes or goals.

How meaning is assigned or information is interpreted depends on individual experiences, values, beliefs, and perceptions. For example, on hearing the words "chair," ten people would likely come up with ten different thoughts and representations. Someone might remember chairing a committee, someone else might imagine a white, wooden chair, and someone else might think of a wheel chair or high chair. NLP gives you the tools to manage your own thoughts and perceptions, as well as improve your communication skills. How does NLP do this? It helps you develop useful thoughts and representations, as well as respond to the different thoughts and representations of others. When you understand that "chair" can represent many different things, you also understand that the meaning and possibility of any given situation will depend on how you represent the information related to that situation. You will also understand that because "chair" represents different things to different people, you must work to understand the perspective of others in communication. Successful management of your thoughts and perceptions allows you to remove blocks on the path to excellence and achievement. NLP also gives you the tools to understand and respond to the thoughts and perceptions of others, thus creating stronger relationships in your professional and personal life.

NLP was developed from the research of Richard Bandler and John Grinder. Bandler and Grinder met at the University of California at Santa Cruz. At the time of their meeting in the 1970s, Bandler was an undergraduate student studying mathematics. Grinder held a doctorate and served as an associate professor in linguistics. They wanted to understand why, in spite of a relatively level playing field — for example, equal education and experience — some therapists enjoyed significantly greater success than did others. Bandler and Grinder examined the behavior of these therapists and isolated several core behaviors they all shared. Bandler and Grinder used these behaviors to understand what made the therapists successful and to teach others how they could experience similar success.

NLP at its core is about modeling human excellence, according to Grinder and Bandler. In other words, it is about copying or emulating someone who has successfully done something you want to do. When you model human excellence, you note which thoughts, behaviors, and resources contribute to success in others and change what you are doing to match what the successful person does. Bandler and Grinder developed NLP to support people in making successful changes in their lives. To make these changes, Grinder and Bandler encouraged people to change what did not working for them and, instead, model patterns that worked for others who had achieved success.

One example of creating change where current thoughts, feelings, or responses were not working involves phobias. During their work with people and problem behavior, Grinder and Bandler noticed that even when they were not in any danger at all, people with phobias experienced fear and other negative emotions. Bandler and Grinder also noticed that people who had successfully overcome phobias had no negative feelings because they learned to see themselves as observers rather than participants during the phobic experience. People bothered by phobias can change or overcome them by modeling human "excellence" — or in this case, copying the behavior of people who have already overcome their phobias. If, for example, just the sight of a spider conjures up feelings of fear, it can help to remember that there are other ways to feel or think about that experience. In this instance, NLP would encourage overcoming a spider phobia by adopting the thoughts and representations of someone who has overcome a fear of spiders.

NLP is useful for anyone who wants to achieve excellence at anything from work or sports performance to relationships and personal confidence. Decades of study on the habits of successful people have yielded a body of research that provides information about what successful people do, how they think and frame things, and how they see themselves. People wanting to achieve success can duplicate that success by applying the same strategies in their own lives.

Much like the blueprints for building a house, NLP provides the guide for taking a vision or a plan from thought to being. Achieving excellence with NLP involves creating change through deliberate integration of minds (both conscious and subconscious or unconscious), language, and behavior. In the simplest terms, as you think, you are. That does not mean becoming a star athlete is simply a matter of visualizing yourself winning a gold medal. It does mean that because you determine what the information you receive means, you can actively work to change meaning, thus changing results.

NLP recognizes that everyone has two minds, one conscious and the other unconscious — or subconscious. (These terms will be used interchangeably in this book.) The practice of NLP involves aligning the minds and engaging the unconscious mind to create desirable changes. Create the life you want by being in charge of your unconscious mind. The subconscious mind significantly influences what you think, how you feel, and what you do. NLP helps you manage your subconscious mind.

Think about it; there have probably been times in your life when your conscious mind had one thought — ask for a raise — but your unconscious mind had another thought —

you will never get a raise; you cannot ask for a raise in this economy; just be glad you have a job; you do not deserve a raise; you do not have the confidence to ask for a raise; it is greedy to ask for a raise. Although your conscious mind may think about a raise, it is unlikely you will act on the thought because your unconscious mind does not believe a raise is possible for you. What you believe on a subconscious level is directly related to what you do. This is why alignment of your conscious and unconscious minds is so important. With alignment, your minds — both conscious and subconscious — language, and behavior all row the boat in the same direction, so to speak. When they row in different directions, you will likely find yourself moving in circles or even backward, instead of straight ahead toward excellence and achievement.

This book offers an easy-to-use guide to NLP, starting with a brief overview of the tools of NLP. Some of the concepts may seem familiar because a number of them have been employed in traditional therapeutic models or are just common sense ideas you have heard before. According to NLP experts Steve Andreas and Charles Faulkner, NLP has been popularized by Anthony Robbins, John Bradshaw, and others. Bits of NLP have found their way into sales trainings, communications seminars, classrooms, and conversations. When anyone talks about modeling human excellence, getting in state, building rapport, creating a compelling future, or how "visual" they are, they refer to concepts from NLP.

You have probably heard the expressions, "Change your mind, change your life" or "Free your mind, and the rest will follow." NLP shows you just how to change and free your mind. Ultimately, your attitude, or how you think about something, significantly impacts how you will experience it.

Again, NLP is not about magic or mystery. It is about the deliberate integration of the conscious and subconscious mind with behavior and language to achieve a carefully considered, or well-formed, outcome. Do not worry if the concepts are not familiar. Each of these will be discussed at length in later sections of the book.

The following are some tips for getting the most from your experience with this book:

- Refer to the definitions and concepts in the quick-start guide as you read the book, and complete the exercises until you are comfortable with each of them.

- Make notes of any goals you want to accomplish. Use the tools in this book to help you form and accomplish your goals.

- Practice each of the ideas and exercises. Keep a journal as you move through the book to chart your progress. You might also consider going through the book with a friend who will hold you accountable for the goals you set and celebrate with you as you accomplish each of them.

- Give particular attention to the case studies included throughout the book. These studies give useful examples from NLP practitioners for achieving results with NLP.

- Be patient with yourself as you work through this book. Remember, your attitude will shape your experience.

Neuro-linguistic Programming Quick-Start Guide

The guide includes a quick overview of NLP basics like concepts, presuppositions, pillars, sense modes, states, and anchors. You will want to refer to this section often while you become familiar with NLP practices and ideas.

The basic concepts of NLP

Create well-formed outcomes to accomplish your goals. This critical concept supports successful outcomes. The steps for developing well-formed outcomes are included in the following list. *Chapter 4 will discuss how to create a well-formed outcome.*

1. Think in terms of what you want; avoid thinking about what you do not want.
2. Create a clear mental picture of what you want; see what you want.
3. Feel yourself experiencing what you want. Make the experience as vividly real as you can; this will become easier with practice.
4. Determine if you have the resources needed to get what you want.

5. Choose to be accountable for what you can control.
6. Anticipate and plan for any obstacles.

Using these concepts aligns both your conscious and subconscious mind with the desired outcome and directs all energy toward its accomplishment.

Some presuppositions of NLP

Presuppositions offer a basis for understanding and changing your thoughts and behavior. *A detailed explanation of the presuppositions is included in Chapter 1.* These presuppositions are commonly held in NLP. The presuppositions of NLP include:

1. The map is not the territory.
2. People respond based on their own individual map.
3. There is no failure, only feedback.
4. The meaning of communication is the response you get.
5. If what you are doing is not working, do something different.
6. You cannot *not* communicate.
7. Individuals have all the resources they need to achieve their desired outcomes.
8. Every behavior has a positive intent.
9. People are much more than their behavior.
10. The mind and body are interlinked and affect each other.
11. Having choice is better than not having choice.
12. Modeling successful performance leads to excellence.

Representation

Representation refers to the mental picture you create upon hearing a cue. What comes to mind when you hear the word "chair" or "car?" Each person will form a different picture based on his or her experiences, values, and ideas. Your representation of things can have a positive or negative effect on your relationships and achievements. Understanding that people represent things differently will help you improve your communication skills.

Pillars

The pillars, or building blocks, of NLP are rapport, outcome thinking, sensory awareness, and behavioral flexibility. Many of the ideas of NLP are based on understanding and working to manage these four basics. *A discussion of these pillars is included in Chapter 2.*

Framing

Framing concerns your perceptions of an event or circumstance and the choices you think are available to you based on those perceptions. In simpler terms, your attitude — how you think and talk about something — has a direct impact on how you feel about it and what you think you can do about it.

VAK

NLP helps you understand that everyone uses three primary sense or sensory modes to communicate and learn. These are:

- **V**isual (or seeing)
- **A**uditory (or hearing)
- **K**inesthetic (or feeling)

The secondary modes of communication are gustatory (taste) and olfactory (smell). Though these are used less often, they can be very important for getting into state or creating powerful visualization experiences.

Recognizing which sense mode you operate from can improve your outcomes. Also, recognizing which sensory mode others operate from can improve rapport. *Chapter 5 includes a discussion of sense modes.*

State

The term state is used to describe, in total, the emotions, thoughts, and feelings you experience in the moment. In other words, the state you are in describes what is going on with and for you internally. For example, you may be in a calm or agitated state. If you are in a state that is dysfunctional or simply not useful, you could use an NLP tool, such as the Circle of Excellence pattern, to break state. Breaking state refers to moving from your current emotional state into another one, most often from a negative or nonproductive place to a more useful one. *Chapter 7 will describe breaking state in more detail, along with the Circle of Excellence.*

Metaprograms

Metaprograms are like the framework or master program that determines your patterns of interaction during communication. In other words, your metaprogram will govern your verbal and non-verbal communication habits. When you change metaprograms, you will notice your communication patterns change as well. Metaprograms also determine what strategies you will choose to get anything done and whether you act on a toward- or away-from motivation. When you take action because you want to avoid something — such as being fired, embarrassed, or unprepared — you use an away-from motivation. Using an away-from motivation means you are motivated to avoid an outcome by completing the action. People motivated in this way take action to avoid the thing they do not want to happen. When you take an action, such as signing up for a class to get a promotion or raise, you use a toward motivation. Using a toward motivation means you are motivated by the outcome or reward you will get on completing the action. People using a toward motivation take action to experience something they want to happen.

Anchoring

An anchor grounds you in the best state for achieving your goals. It is a signal or reminder to assume a posture or attitude for success. For example, if each time you feel calm and relaxed you fold your hands together, you reinforce feelings of calm and relaxation. The feeling and the action become associated in your mind so the next time you feel anxious, folding your hands together should restore you to a state of calm. In this example, folding your hands together is called firing the anchor. If you become calm, you have been successful in triggering the desired state. You can also set up anchors unintentionally or trigger an unwanted state. For example, say that each time you hear a particular word or phrase you become angry. When this happens, you can learn to change your response by extinguishing the anchor. *This will be discussed further in Chapter 2.*

Chapter 1

WHAT IS NEURO-LINGUISTIC PROGRAMMING?

Neuro-linguistic programming provides a framework for understanding how people construct subjective experience and the tools to reconstruct that experience when necessary. Using these tools, you can take what you have learned (if what you have learned prevents a desired change or outcome), unlearn it, and learn something more useful. In other words, NLP shows you how to produce a desired change or outcome. NLP is the study of modeling and creating excellence in our lives.

Many people have learned communication skills that are not useful because the skills do not help them achieve their desired outcomes. If you ever had a manager who came off as impatient and gruff or just plain unlikeable, you have seen an example of someone who is a good candidate for unlearning and relearning a style of communication. Such a person may have learned to use words and body language to exert power over others rather than to build rapport with them. He or she can relearn new skills.

The Four Learning Levels of NLP

Learning a new skill happens in four phases or levels of competence. The levels take the learner from beginner to expert as knowledge and confidence grows. The four levels of learning are called subconscious incompetence, conscious incompetence, conscious competence, and subconscious competence. An explanation of each follows.

Subconscious incompetence

At the subconscious incompetence level, the learner not only does not have the skill, but also the learner does not know of his or her skill deficit. Using the example of the manager, he or she will continue to communicate poorly until becoming aware of the problem and making a choice to improve.

Conscious incompetence

At the conscious incompetence level, the learner begins to understand the skill deficit exists but does not yet have command of the skill. Our manager now understands his or her communication style gets in the way of his or her professional goals of building rapport, morale, and productivity among employees.

Conscious competence

At the conscious competence level, the learner develops the skill. Imagine learning to ride a bike. The learner may feel a bit wobbly and is aware of trying very hard to ride without falling. The manager now tries to understand how others respond to his or her communication style and begins to adapt his or her behavior so the results support his or her professional goals. He or she is learning to create rapport.

Subconscious competence

Finally, at the subconscious competence level, the learner has fully mastered the skill. The behavior has become ingrained and automatic. Without thinking now, our manager picks up and responds to subtle facial cues, voice tones, and verbal and nonverbal language in interacting with others. He or she can positively influence others and no longer relies on fear as a management tool.

Review the levels again using the manager as the learner. At the beginning level of subconscious incompetence, the manager does not understand that his or her communication style is off-putting. He or she cannot figure out why employees resist his or her wishes for cooperation or why employees misunderstand him or her.

Wanting to improve, the manager may ask for feedback. The manager has reached conscious incompetence. He or she knows that his or her communication style is at the root of the problem but does not yet have the skills to improve the style.

Next, the manager becomes consciously competent. He or she uses feedback information to practice communication strategies that build rapport and reduce resistance. The skills are emerging and are not yet automatic or "second nature" because the learner consciously works to develop new communications skills.

With time, the manager becomes subconsciously competent. He or she uses new verbal and nonverbal cues to create connections with employees. The new skill has become a habit patterned in his or her brain. The manager has become so comfortable with these skills that they are as natural as brushing his or her teeth. Subconscious competence indicates mastery of a skill. The learner can now use the new skills without conscious thought, or subconsciously, because they are second nature. Once a skill has been mastered, it moves to a lower center of the brain, making room in the higher brain for new learning.

History of NLP

John Grinder and Richard Bandler share credit for creating neuro-linguistic programming (NLP). NLP is based on their study of language patterns used by Frederick (Fritz)

Perls and Laura Perls, founders of Gestalt therapy; Virginia Satir, considered the mother of family therapy; Gregory Bateson, philosopher; and Milton Erickson, a psychiatrist and renowned hypnotherapist.

An often controversial figure, Richard Bandler was born in 1950. He holds both a Bachelor of Arts and Master of Arts in psychology. It was research on therapists, such as Gestalt and Satir who inspired Bandler, who was initially devoted to mathematics and computer science, to pursue degrees in psychology. Bandler's controversies rise from a period of heavy cocaine use and suspicion of murder. He was acquitted on charges of murder. Grinder was born in 1940 and holds a Bachelor of Arts in psychology and a doctorate in linguistics.

Bandler and Grinder met at the University of California at Santa Cruz (UCSC) where they led weekly Gestalt therapy groups in the mid-1970s for UCSC students. Gestalt therapy helps people separate thoughts and feelings caused by what happens in the present moment from those left over from the past. According to Gary Yontef, Ph.D., in his book *Awareness, Dialogue, and Process*, Gestalt therapy focuses more on process — what is happening — than content — what is being discussed. Gestalt therapy emphasizes what is being done, thought, and felt at the moment rather than on what was, might be, could be, or should be.

Initial Gestalt therapy groups emulated founder Fritz Perls as closely as possible, from his accent and communication style to his habit of smoking. Bandler and Grinder used their theory of modeling human excellence with the goal of isolating the behaviors that led to Perls' success. Identifying and isolating behaviors helped the men understand which ones they should keep and which ones they could discard, such as the smoking.

Grinder and Bandler duplicated this process with other therapists, such as Virginia Satir. Satir, a founder of family therapy and instrumental in the creation of the first family therapy program in the United States, believed that family and therapeutic relationships would be more successful when they emphasized love, nurturing, and warmth. Satir thought many people hold onto beliefs that served them at one time, such as when they were children, but later held them back. She taught people how to move beyond beliefs that were not useful to create deeper and richer life experiences.

From this research, Grinder and Bandler learned many things that would form the foundation of neuro-linguistic programming. For example, they noticed the successful therapists used similar linguistic patterns. Linguistic, or language, patterns include things like speech, grammar, sentence structure, and word phrasing. They also noticed the therapists responded to clients using the client's representational system. For example, if the client used a visual representational system, the therapist might use responses like, "It is clear to me" or "I see what you mean." Bandler's master's thesis, which was eventually published in 1975 as volume one of *The Structure of Magic*, is based on findings from these research groups. A follow-up, *The Structure of Magic, Vol. 2*, was published the following year.

Grinder and Bandler expounded on their early work by studying Milton Erickson. As a young man, Erickson was diagnosed with polio. He spent more than a year in an iron lung — a respirator that encloses the entire body, except the head, and helps with breathing. After his time in the chamber, still bedridden, Erickson watched family and friends closely. Through sharp observation, he taught himself to interpret and understand the conscious and unconscious ways people behave and relate. Erickson would later use his observations to revolutionize the fields of psychotherapy and hypnosis. Bandler and Grinder used Erickson's work to teach people how to understand and duplicate excellence in their own lives.

Part of creating excellence is recognizing the patterns people have in place that yield undesirable results. With NLP, the problem is not the person; people work perfectly. The problem is the pattern of thinking, feeling, and doing. When people engage their patterns, they consistently get the same results. If they do not like the results, they must change the pattern. Your job in modeling human excellence is to learn what patterns successful people use and employ them in your own life. You need not understand why you engage a particular pattern. It is enough to understand how to change the pattern. The presuppositions of NLP help you understand how to change the pattern.

The Milton Model

The Milton model refers to language patterns used to alter a state of consciousness or create a trance. Milton Erickson did this by omitting or generalizing some of the details normally included when sharing information. When the information is missing, the listener must search within for the meaning not verbally conveyed. This is called a transderivational search (TDS). That search leads the listener to focus on internal representations instead of what happens externally. This process induces trance, and in this place, the listener is most receptive to suggestions.

Presuppositions of NLP

Neuro-linguistic programming is based on a number of tenets or ideas that provide the basis for understanding how to manage the mind to achieve excellence. Many of these assumptions challenge thought patterns that keep people stuck and unable to accomplish their most cherished goals. Each presupposition provides an alternative perspective from which to view formerly limiting thoughts and experiences. It is a good idea to review the presuppositions when facing challenges with meeting a goal or developing a new skill. These are the most common guiding principles of NLP.

The map is not the territory

This statement coined by Alfred Korzybski, a mathematician, has its origins in the field of general semantics (GS). According to the Institute of General Semantics (**www.**

generalsemantics.org), general semantics "provides a systematic methodology to understand how you relate to the world around you, how you react to this world, how you react to your reactions, and how you may adjust your behavior accordingly." Your understanding of the world around you and how you choose to respond to the world is based on individual maps.

In NLP, the map is like a software program governing what you think, say, and do. As in the world of technology, software programs vary widely. The map can only be a partial representation of the actual possible territory, which is vast. In other words, one person's map can never fully express what is. The map can only express information filtered through an individual's perceptions.

Think of a modified game of Scrabble® as an example. Four players get the same seven letters, making more than one hundred words possible. One player might see 20 different word possibilities that he or she can spell using the letters. Another might see only one word, another might see 55, and the last player may not find any words among the letters at all. As players gain more skill and knowledge, they can see more possible words among the letters. Until they gain more skill and knowledge, the number of possible words they see will be limited. It is important to remember that the word possibilities — the territory — exist whether or not they are recognized — on the map — by the players.

People respond based on their individual map

Everyone has his or her own individual map for the world. This map is drawn as he or she collects information through the senses — visual (sight), auditory (hearing), kinesthetic (feeling), olfactory (smelling), and gustatory (tasting) — and interprets it based on his or her own values, beliefs, and background. Much of that information settles in the subconscious mind without the individual's conscious awareness. He or she uses information from his or her conscious and subconscious minds to form beliefs, feelings, and values. This information also governs his or her actions.

Even though everyone has their own different map, the true reality of the world is the same. Think back to the Scrabble game. Just because you do not see the word possibilities does not mean they do not exist. Peoples' maps are different because their perceptions are different. Thoughts, actions, and behaviors are based on mental maps. For example, one person might see a dog and think danger and freeze or run. Another person might see the same dog and feel flooded with warm feelings and reach down to tousle its fur.

With an understanding that the map is not the territory comes an awareness that a variety of responses are possible in a given situation. If your current response is not useful to you or your desired outcomes, recognizing that the map is not the territory allows you to redraw the lines of your map and chart a different behavior course. You can change the world, as you experience it, by changing your map.

There is no failure — only feedback

Language matters not just when you talk to others but when you talk to yourself, too. When you attempt to do something and find that your results do not match your anticipated outcome, it is most useful to view the experience as one you can learn from rather than one that was wasted or failed. If you choose to regard the experience in this way, you will look for information you can use in re-working your anticipated outcome, such as lining up originally overlooked resources, making a secondary plan for navigating obstacles, or planning how you will talk yourself through moments of fear, doubt, and hesitation.

Failures or Feedback?

Consider the following list of "failures:"

1831: Lost job
1832: Lost bid for Illinois State Legislature
1833: Lost a business
1835: Lost a sweetheart
1836: Suffered a nervous breakdown
1838: Lost a bid for Illinois House Speaker
1843: Lost a bid for nomination to U.S. Congress
1849: Not chosen for land officer job
1854: Lost bid for the Senate
1856: Lost bid to become U.S. Vice President
1858: Lost another bid for the Senate

This list of failures belongs to Abraham Lincoln, elected 16th president of the United States in 1860. Today, Lincoln is regarded as one of the most admired and respected presidents ever. Imagine if he had allowed himself to become paralyzed or stagnant each time he did not accomplish his desired outcome. When considering your own so-called failures, it is important to do as Lincoln did and keep moving toward the desired outcome. When you understand that you should regard these experiences as feedback, you begin to realize that failures should not paralyze or discourage; instead, they should energize ongoing efforts.

Evaluating feedback rather than chalking up failure fosters feelings of control and possibility. So rather than saying, "I will never be able to lose weight because I always fail with diet and exercise," you can review and rework past plans. For example, maybe you had a great exercise plan but child care fell through or you caught a cold and lost momentum when you did not feel well. Using that feedback, you might rework your plan by buying an exercise video or trampoline instead of a gym membership, choosing a gym that offers child care, or enlisting the support of an exercise buddy who will hold you accountable and encourage you to continue your exercise plan as soon as you feel better. The key here is what you tell yourself about why you did not accomplish your goal and how you use what you tell yourself to change the outcome. Try the following exercise.

EXERCISE 1:
TURN FAILURE
INTO FEEDBACK

What should you do when your efforts do not result in the desired outcome? Look for the lesson, evaluate what did happen, and look for ways to use that information to improve future outcomes. The following exercise can be useful for shifting your thoughts about the experience from failure to opportunity for feedback.

Step 1: Spend a few minutes reviewing your feelings. What are you thinking? How do you feel? Which of these thoughts and attitudes feels like the one causing the problem? How is the thought represented in your mind? How does the thought make you feel?

> *Example:* How this step might look: You bombed your last job interview. You may have felt embarrassed, worried, incompetent, fearful, or just plain stupid. Now, you are preparing for another interview, and it seems impossible to get your nerves under control. Is your fear that the interview might not go well paralyzing you and jangling your nerves? Do you feel yourself shaking as you imagine what the interviewers will think about you?

Step 2: Challenge your thinking about the interview experience. Is it possible to interview well even if you do not have the perfect answer for every question? What else were you thinking and feeling? Perhaps you were feeling capable and confident until the interviewer introduced a topic you are not familiar with.

Step 3: Stay with the feelings you had before the topic that made you feel uncomfortable was introduced. See yourself hearing the difficult topic and remaining in your capable and confident state. What responses will you offer? What thoughts are going through your mind?

Step 4: Create an anchor. It should allow you to remain relaxed even if you do not know the answer to a question. See yourself firing the anchor and triggering the state that allows you to respond calmly and without panic during the interview. Examples of an anchor might include folding your hands together. If you consistently fold your hands together when you are feeling calm and relaxed, for example during prayer or meditation, the very act of folding your hands together will become associated with a calm state and thus become calming. When you fold your hands during a stressful situation, you are said to be firing the anchor. If you begin to feel calm, you have triggered the desired state.

The meaning of communication is the response it gets

This presupposition is especially useful for parents of teenagers. Parents intend to communicate love and concern. Teens hear angry, frustrated badgering, and of course, they respond in kind. The original message — such as "I care about what happens to you, and I want you to be safe" — is lost amidst hurt and angry feelings, and in extreme cases, the relationship begins to suffer.

If it seems you are constantly misunderstood or listener responses demonstrate they took away a meaning you did not intend, you can improve. Notice that the emphasis here is on improving rather than blaming. If someone is not understanding you, you can take responsibility for the miscommunication and take action to clarify your meaning. The bonus? Better relationships.

NLP not only helps you model the excellence of others, it helps you duplicate your own success. Parents who have trouble communicating with teens may have excellent communication skills with co-workers or in other settings. If you are getting the responses you want and being understood in some settings, think about why. What are you doing and saying in those settings? If you have trouble communicating in all settings, do not worry — you can find success.

Think about the person you are trying to communicate with. Watch for and listen to his or her responses for clues about how the conversation is going. What do you know about this person? What cues can you pick up from facial expressions? What can you say to facilitate understanding? Is it a matter of changing your words, tone, delivery, or physical proximity? Is it a matter of listening more? By paying attention as you communicate, you can make subtle changes to repair a disconnect or reinforce a connection.

If what you are doing is not working, do something different

This concept seems simple enough when you read it, but is it really? People can find multiple examples of things they do that they know do not work. Do any of these sound familiar? You wait until the last minute to buy or send birthday cards so they always arrive late; you put off that paper or presentation until the last minute and then get it done but know you could have done better; you spend outside of your budget; you confide in people who are not trustworthy; or you race around with the kids before school so everyone starts the day feeling cranky and frazzled. The examples of how people all continue to do things that do not work are endless.

Most people have at least one place where they would benefit greatly by doing something different. No matter how long you have had a habit or behavior, it is not permanent. Simply recognizing this can open you to the possibility that you *can* do something different. Behavior can be changed. Dr. Sandra Chapman, founder of the Center for BrainHealth at The University of Texas at Dallas, believes the brain is among the most modifiable parts of the human body. People know from scientific research that adult brains are, indeed, malleable. Like child brains, adult brains are also capable of generating change and new cells. This phenomenon, called neuroplasticity, means that new experiences can change neurons — the nerve cells in the brain — and how they are organized. What does that mean for you? No matter how long you have had a habit, even if it has been decades, the brain can adapt and develop new patterns for new habits.

You cannot not communicate

Communication is more than what you say; it is both verbal *and* nonverbal. Everything about you, from your clothes to your body language, communicates a message. For example, how might you express interest in what a person says without verbalizing your interest? How can you tell if someone feels worried, confident, happy, or angry? People use language, facial expressions, and body cues that reveal something about the way they think and feel. They express themselves many different ways, including through choice of words and style of dress.

When it comes to communication, one of the goals is congruence. Congruence happens when your subconscious and conscious mind are aligned. That alignment helps you present a consistent message because what you say matches what you do. You are said to be incongruent when what you say does not match what you do. During communication, an example of incongruence might be saying you are interested in what a person is saying but checking text messages, shuffling papers, or letting your mind wander while he or she talks. Your words indicate one message: "I am interested in what you are saying," but your behavior communicates a different message: "I have more interesting or important things to do than listen to what you are saying."

Individuals have all the resources they need to achieve their desired outcomes

Everyone has the power to create change in his or her own life. An expression says, "Even a broken clock is right twice each day." Applied to individuals, the expression could be interpreted to mean that everyone, no matter the circumstance, has a strong and perfect place from which to build. Accepting the idea that individuals have all the resources they need requires you to search for those resources in themselves and others, no matter how deeply they are hidden. This presupposition allows you to change your interpretation of some behaviors and reconsider others. For example, suppose you have tried to lose weight in the past without success. The problem is not the goal or your ability to accomplish it; it is your willingness to understand how to direct your internal resources toward accomplishing the goal.

Underlying every behavior is a positive intent

The presupposition that underlying every behavior is a positive intent is not a license to commit or reason to condone bad behavior. Examples of bad behavior include bullying, hitting, yelling, stealing, and lying. Consider the legendary English hero Robin Hood who is said to have robbed from the rich — negative behavior — to give to the poor — positive intent. When you uncover the underlying positive intention behind bad behavior — wanting to belong or feel included, wanting to be heard, or warding off danger or hunger, for example — you can look for and adopt new behaviors to support the intention. In your own life, this would mean looking for the reward or payoff you get for bad behavior. You must then look for positive ways to get the same or a better payoff so your behavior change is supported. This presupposition invites you to have more compassion for others and yourself by making it possible to separate the deed from the doer. This presupposition also helps you understand behavior and develop appropriate motivation for changing behavior you no longer want.

People are much more than their behavior

Most people have heard about separating the deed from the doer. Individuals are quite complex and cannot be fully understood just by what they do. Sometimes, behaviors are contradictory or happen only in limited or extreme circumstances. Think of a religious leader who has profoundly touched hundreds of lives but who has also misappropriated hundreds of dollars. Some behavior represents only a glimmer of what is really possible. Think of a student with above-average intelligence who consistently underperforms. You are more than what you do because the possibilities for what you can do are limitless. Behavior is or can be always changing. It is not fixed. Understanding that people are much more than their behavior helps you know you are not limited by what you have done. The ability to remove limits by doing something different or better is always available to you.

People make the best choices available to them

You may wonder how people end up in jail, work jobs they hate, or wind up with addictions. Everyone makes choices based on his or her own individual history, values, beliefs, and experiences. People do the best they can with what they believe is available to them. They bring their own unique worldview and perception to each decision they make. In some cases, their worldview obscures the full range of possibilities, leaving them to select from limited choices. When you remember that the map is not the territory, you understand that you can broaden your worldview or rework your maps to add more choices. Remember that even when you do not see a choice, there likely is one there that will become visible with a different map or a different perspective. You have probably experienced this when you explained a problem to a friend who offered you a perspective or solution that never even occurred to you.

Consider this take on perspective around priorities.

Big Rocks

At a workshop on setting priorities, the facilitator asked each participant to talk a little about what he or she hoped to gain during the next two hours.

Many people talked about feeling overwhelmed, stressed, and like they were running in place. No matter how busy they were or how fast they ran, they just could not seem to do the things that really needed to get done. There just do not seem to be enough hours in the day, several people lamented.

Overwhelmingly, those present in the room sought ideas and support for achieving work-life balance. They wanted to know the magic formula for "doing it all."

Much of what was discussed that afternoon was based on Stephen Covey's *The 7 Habits of Highly Effective People*. The focus was on two habits specifically: "Put first things first" and "Begin with the end in mind."

Using those habits as a springboard, participants spent a good bit of time crafting the beginnings of a personal mission statement. Like the mission statements created in boardrooms or for business plans, personal mission statements can help clarify, direct, and motivate. These statements can also help prioritize or identify what Covey calls "Big Rocks" — those things that are most important to you, such as your relationship with your partner or children or time in the garden.

When you begin to distinguish your Big Rocks from the little rocks in your life, it becomes easier to order your priorities accordingly. Little rocks are the things that might be important but might not move you closer to your life purpose or goals. They might not be important for any reason other than to keep you busy or protect you from the discomfort of saying "no" if you are not good at setting boundaries. To illustrate this point, the facilitator showed a clip from a Covey workshop.

In the clip, an audience member comes to the stage. She is presented with a bucket nearly full of little rocks. Several big rocks sat on the table beside the bucket, and beside that was an empty bucket.

Her challenge: Get all the rocks in one bucket. She tried hard. The woman pushed little rocks this way and that, she shifted and turned the big rocks, she puzzled and persevered, but she could not make them all fit in the bucket.

After many diligent attempts, the solution came to her. She put each of the big rocks in the empty bucket, and then she arranged the little rocks to fit around the big rocks.

In what ways does your current perspective on a situation keep you from meeting your priorities?

Modeling successful performance leads to excellence

Modeling successful performance shows that if one person can do something, anyone can learn to do it. Perhaps your results will not be identical — you may not become a multimillion-dollar motivational speaker like Tony Robbins, for example — but you will get significantly higher evaluation feedback for your workshop presentations. Unlike more traditional psychology, NLP is not concerned with describing the problems you experience or uncovering why you have problems. With NLP, you would not focus on why you are paralyzed by stage fright before you present. NLP is instead concerned with how incoming information is processed and interpreted to create the current experience. When someone experiences success, people can duplicate that success by understanding how his or her thoughts, actions, and feelings came together to produce that success. You can then apply those patterns in your own life. Obviously, there will be times that physical or environmental limits change your outcomes. Still, you will have enhanced your capacity by creating new patterns of experience when you model someone who is successful.

The Growth of NLP

NLP was a new idea in the 1970s. Today, it is the subject of hundreds of seminars, articles, CDs, DVDs, and books. Some of the best known of these books include Tony Robbins' *Unlimited Power: The New Science of Personal Achievement; Change Your Mind and Keep The Change; and Frogs*

Into Princes; and transcripts of Bandler and Grinder's seminars edited by Steve and Connirae Andreas. There are also dozens of NLP training centers located around the world. Researchers and practitioners continue to discover new applications and strategies in the quest for excellence. Although NLP has encountered some skepticism in mainstream psychology, Researchers and practitioners alike have documented many real life examples of change. This book is written in the hope that you, too, will find what you need to create the changes you want in your life.

Criticism of NLP

Though the number of proponents has grown since its development by Bandler and Grinder, NLP is not without detractors. NLP has not enjoyed the same mainstream acceptance as other disciplines, such as psychotherapy. This is, in part, owed to the fact that NLP has not been largely embraced by academicians providing the type of in-depth research that leads to their stamp of approval. Wider acceptance of NLP has also been hampered by what can only be called a fringe element. NLP offers very accessible concepts and ideas, such as using rapport to influence behavior, which a few people have taken and misused. As a result, some people hold the mistaken impression that NLP is about wild mind tricks designed to take advantage of people and part them from their money. Readers should be reminded that an opportunity for abuse exists in any field. There is also opportunity. NLP offers useful tools for understanding and managing your own behavior and enjoying better relationships.

Why NLP is Not More Popular

NLP training organizations have hurt themselves and the NLP field in an important way: They have had a long-time pattern of trying to "be all things to all people," which is a turn off to corporate buyers and many individuals. NLP is applicable across many disciplines. A doctor or dentist can use it to help with pain and stress management during surgical procedures. A teacher can use it to create rapport in the classroom or to understand why a student may struggle with the coursework. Behavioral health professionals can utilize it to understand clients better and to help them make lasting behavioral changes. Business people can use it in a variety of ways. It is even used in spiritual circles. Put a teacher, a dentist, a corporate executive, a shaman, and a psychologist in the same study group — and well, you have to admit, that would look a little suspect to a corporate leader being asked to sign off on an educational reimbursement expense. Whether consciously or unconsciously, buyers ask, "With so many disparate professions mixed in the same class, will I truly get something that I can bring back to my environment?" The answer is yes, but it is not obvious.

In addition, the name is off-putting: neuro-linguistic programming. Some people think, "No, thank you. I do not want to be programmed." And the pattern names, such as "Core Transformation" and "Six-step Reframing" might be perfect for a psychotherapist but not for a corporate executive.

It takes a leap of faith to fork out money for this training. NLP should be wildly popular. If people truly understood its benefits, NLP would be required education in many professions.

CASE STUDY:
SUCCESSFUL USE OF NLP

Judith E. Pearson, Ph.D.
Licensed professional counselor
Motivational Strategies, Inc.
judy@engagethepower.com
www.engagethepower.com

I took my first practitioner training in 1988 and have practiced NLP since then. I have practitioner, master practitioner, and trainer certifications in NLP, with more than 17 years of teaching NLP and more than 20 years of using it in my practice as a licensed professional counselor. I teach for various organizations around the Washington, D.C. area, such as the American Hypnosis Training Academy and Ultimate Success Coaching. I have also written around 100 book reviews on NLP and hypnosis since 1997.

I use NLP principles in my practice and in teaching NLP as a practical guide to understanding human behavior, explaining what I do, and in my choice of NLP interventions. I conduct individual therapy and coaching mostly with adults and occasionally with adolescents. I work with behavioral, emotional, health, and performance issues.

In terms of who can benefit from NLP, I think anyone older than the age of 5 with average, or better, intelligence can benefit from some aspect of NLP. In fact, most people can learn NLP principles on their own. People can benefit from the skills of a practitioner by learning the patterns, strategies, and communication skills. NLP provides a framework for many different approaches to behavioral change, and each practitioner can adapt NLP to his or her own style and the needs of his or her clientele.

Each NLP session is unique because I use it to address a wide range of issues. I often combine various forms of hypnosis with NLP. Usually, my sessions include a well-formed outcome and an NLP pattern to help the client access resources or new decisions, understandings, or strategies regarding the problem at hand.

I remain very formal with the patterns, although I might add my own variations. I think the intuitive part comes about from empathy and rapport — an unconscious connection between myself and the client that tells me what to say when.

Although many people make a distinction between NLP and hypnotherapy, I do not see much difference between them. I purposely use trance work in NLP. However, because most laypeople are not familiar with the benefits of NLP, I advertise my services as a hypnotherapist. Therefore, many of my clients have the expectation that they will get to experience what one client referred to as a "real hypnosis," in which they simply lean back, close their eyes, and let me do most of the talking. For these sessions, I take the more traditional approach, with a formal trance induction, deepening, and direct suggestions. I might also add in guided imagery, mental rehearsal, reframing, and NLP patterns.

I think the most important benefit of NLP is it is experiential for clients: They participate in the process through visualization, revivification of memories, accessing internal resources, following new strategies, and mental rehearsal. They actually get to experience the changes taking place throughout the session. A common denominator for what people are looking for is help to do the one thing they want to do but do not or cannot bring themselves to do.

NLP is so ingrained in my thinking that I use it automatically, without planning or conscious awareness I am doing it. NLP has given me a solution-orientation to every challenge I face. NLP has also become the way I earn my living. NLP has significantly improved my interpersonal skills.

I follow the NLP model to build and use rapport, which means matching and mirroring, pacing and leading, and communicating empathically. I also believe anchoring is critical to the NLP process. Anchoring helps the client access a resourceful state in which he or she can then implement solutions to the presented problem. This matters because people cannot solve a problem within the parameters of the problem. They have to do something different that they have not experienced before.

I use both the meta model and the Milton model because each serves a purpose in the context of counseling and coaching. The meta model is useful for gathering information and often for inviting the client to think about the problem in a new way. I use the Milton model when doing trance work or when I want the client to respond in a unique way as a result of transderivational search, such as when I want clients to arrive at their own interpretations and meanings of what I say.

I do not agree that NLP is not supported by science. NLP has been subjected to some experimental studies and found to be effective. Moreover, NLP incorporates elements of methods and approaches that have been shown in experimental studies to be highly effective in behavioral change, including rapport, empathy, imagery, trance work, and mental rehearsal.

With NLP, I have success nearly every day I am in sessions with my clients. Recently, I worked with a highly depressed client. She was off work on disability leave for depression and recently returned to her job. Her interpersonal communication skills with co-workers were not as good as they could have been, which was a continuing problem for her, and she had low self-esteem. I helped her mentally rehearse how to relate to co-workers from a resourceful state. At one point she said, "I'm always afraid I'll fail — no matter what I do."

I rejoined with the NLP principle that all failure is feedback containing useful information, and it says nothing about her worth as a person. This was a conversational reframe. I continued talking, but apparently, she heard nothing I said after that. She became very silent and just stared at me. When I stopped talking she said, "I just realized something. I am not the sum total of all my failures." She said this with great exuberance and repeated it. It was a life-changing moment for her. This client said to me on our third session, "I've spent three years in cognitive therapy learning how broken I was, and in three sessions with you, I've got a whole new outlook on life."

Chapter 2

WHAT CAN YOU DO WITH NLP?

Perhaps a better question is what can you not do with NLP? The short answer is, not much. NLP is universally applicable because it is concerned with individual subjective experience. Although feelings and experiences vary widely from person to person, both are experienced by every person.

You can use NLP for any task concerned with self-improvement or individual change. This includes improving confidence, reducing anxiety, delivering better presentations, eliminating unwanted behaviors, and enjoying deeper relationships. You can also use NLP to move past painful trauma and difficult memories. NLP can be successful across a variety of circumstances because it helps you modify your thoughts and perceptions. Thoughts and perceptions are subjective and can be reinterpreted. The reinterpretation helps you release much of the negative feeling around bad experiences and unmet goals.

Many of the tools and ideas of NLP have long held a place in therapy, where they are used alongside more traditional methods. What makes NLP so exciting is its immediate application. You do not have to wait years to see and feel a difference in your life. NLP sessions are time limited and have a specific goal, such as unlearning a fear of snakes, quitting smoking, managing stress, or improving performance. Changes can take place in just one 30-minute session. The focus with NLP is not on diagnosis — "why" is not what matters. The focus is on change — how are you going to create more useful thoughts and behaviors? NLP is not concerned with replacement behavior. Instead, it supports the extinction of non-useful behavior.

During NLP sessions, clients have the opportunity to identify problems or concerns as they see them. You can also do this at home. Remember, NLP is about subjective experience. You are the authority on your thoughts and feelings. Conversations between the client and practitioner or therapist focus on what happens now and what the client would like to happen in the future. Therapists help clients uncover this information using respectful curiosity. Respectful curiosity is a kind of active listening that facilitates discovery for the client. As the process unfolds, the client is invited to step into the feelings and experiences of accomplishing his or her desired goal. Again, you can also do this at home; use your journal as you process what is happening, and plan what you would like to happen. So, what can you do with NLP? Develop more useful ways of thinking, doing, and being that achieve the outcomes you really want.

The Power of Beliefs

Emily Sands, an economics student who studied at Princeton and Harvard, conducted a yearlong study on gender bias in the theater. Sands conducted three studies. In the second of these studies, Sands provided literary managers and artistic directors throughout the country with the same scripts. The only difference in these scripts was the name of the author. Half of the scripts carried the name of a male writer and the other half carried the name of a female writer. Sands found that in spite of the fact that the scripts were absolutely identical, those scripts that appeared to be written by a female author were rated consistently lower.

What does this study suggest about the power of beliefs? Our beliefs function much like the lines on the road or highway. We stay within the boundaries of the lines, even when the boundaries confine us or limit us, because we do not see anything else. NLP allows us to expand the boundaries of our beliefs and create new possibilities that remove non-useful limits.

What Do You Want NLP to Do for You?

Recall the presupposition, "Everyone has the resources they need to make the changes they want." from When you are ready to begin creating changes in your life, it is enough to start by embracing that realization. It does not matter if you have not yet identified or connected with the resources. Just know they are there.

This chapter includes several brief exercises you can practice to begin seeing a difference today. Why not give it a try? You have the resources to learn about and practice NLP. If you want a jump-start, a therapist or NLP practitioner can work with you to understand how you construct reality and reconstruct those values, thoughts, and beliefs that have not been useful.

Whether you realize it or not, you have probably been exposed to some of the ideas of NLP. These ideas regularly flow from the airwaves and throughout corporate and professional settings. Even more than in therapeutic and corporate settings, NLP has been a powerful contributor to the personal development and motivation phenomenon. Anthony "Tony" Robbins, motivational speaker and author of several books, asserts that personal development and accomplishment requires clarity about personal standards — deciding what you do and do not want in your life. In addition to deciding what you want, Robbins advises believing you can have what you want. These ideas are based on NLP, which understands belief to be the foundation for excellence and accomplishment. Beliefs must be aligned in support of your goals because everything you think, feel, and do is based on what you believe about yourself and your world. Not sure beliefs determine what you think, feel, and do? Read the following for a funny example.

Look for the Belief Behind the Behavior

James A. Scott, Ph.D., former pastor of Bethany Baptist Church in Newark, New Jersey, shared this story with the congregation many years ago. It provides a good example of something that happens to all of us. We see or hear something and accept it, unquestioned, as a belief or value.

Laura always prepares her pot roast by first cutting it into two pieces just the way her mother did. Laura's mother, Karen, learned to cut her pot roast in two by watching her mother, Hattie. Laura and Karen observed and adopted this practice, without question, until Laura's 3-year-old daughter wondered why she cut the roast as she was. Like most of us do when considering our own behavior, Laura answered she has always prepared pot roast this way — just like her mother and grandmother. Laura later asked her own mother this question, and she gave a similar answer. Finally, they asked Hattie about her habit of cutting the pot roast in two. Imagine their surprise when Hattie answered that she only cut the pot roast in two because she did not have a pan large enough to keep the meat in one piece.

What behaviors or beliefs are you ready to question? How might these behaviors be limiting you? Remember again the NLP presupposition that the map is not the territory. In other words, with more information or resources, we are free to make new choices that previously seemed unavailable to us.

The power of NLP is in the tools it gives us to eliminate beliefs that are not useful. Engaging both your conscious and subconscious minds helps you identify and discard beliefs that sabotage your efforts to meet your most cherished goals. Have you ever wondered why you could not meet some of your goals? It is chiefly because behavior is tied to thought. You cannot act — no matter how much willpower you have — unless your subconscious mind believes the action you want to undertake is possible for you. Your subconscious mind is as important to your body as the engine or transmission is to your car.

In addition to giving you the tools to align your subconscious mind with your conscious mind and behavior, NLP gives you powerful strategies for problem solving. Again, visiting an NLP practitioner can be helpful, but it is not required to find relief from troublesome issues. Working on your own at home, you might try a simple exercise like observing and questioning your own behavior. For example, suppose you notice that each time your spouse suggests you take a ballroom dance class together, you come up with some excuse about why the class is a bad idea. Question yourself to determine whether you are offering a valid reason to avoid the class — such as, "It would be tough to find time to prepare for my quarterly meeting" — or an excuse that comes from a limiting thought — such as, "I could never learn the steps, and I will look foolish." Most people look foolish when they try something new. Take the questioning one step further to determine which beliefs you have in place about looking foolish. How does this belief impact your feelings about yourself and what you can do?

Another very easy exercise to try at home follows.

EXERCISE 2: CHANGING YOUR MAP OF AN EXPERIENCE

The following is a technique you can use to change bothersome feelings. This strategy for problem solving employs some of the techniques used with behavioral therapy. This is a very easy exercise to try at home.

Step 1: Recreate an experience where you felt ashamed, humiliated, or angry. Imagine yourself having that experience right now. Step into every detail of that event, engaging your senses as you feel the experience. Name the primary feeling that comes to you as accurately as you can. Now, assign the feeling a number on a scale from 1 to 10, with 10 being the most intense.

Step 2: Choose a song that expresses a feeling completely unlike the feeling you experienced during the event. Children's songs often work great because they are light, silly, upbeat, or fun.

Step 3: Now, step back into that same experience. Only this time, hear the silly or happy song you choose playing in the background. Again, make the experience as vivid as you can. Let the music play loud and clear. You may even have to struggle to hear people talking over the music, or you may be so distracted by the bouncy tune that you give more attention to the song than to what is happening..

Step 4: Vividly imagine yourself having the experience once more. This time, imagine the scene without the music. Notice any changes in your feelings. Many people notice the unpleasant feeling has shifted. It may not feel as serious or hurtful. You may even feel that you can laugh about the event now. Check your rating again on a scale from 1 to 10, with 10 being the most intense. Has the number moved at all? If you notice no changes, do not worry. Continue the exercise using different songs — do not be afraid to try wacky or animal sounds — until you find one that helps you release the unpleasant feeling.

Pretty easy, right? The key here is to give yourself over to or step into the experience as if it is happening in the moment. Have you ever heard the expression, "If I had it to do over..."? This exercise provides an opportunity to have the experience again to change the outcome or at least your internal coding of it. Changing your internal coding of the experience changes the way you think and feel about what happened.

You are already on your way to making the changes you want. Read on to learn about other techniques used in NLP to help you access and operate from your most useful state. When you are ready, give one a try.

Using dissociation to eliminate fear

Many people are afraid of spiders and bugs. In most cases, there is no basis for this fear. Think about it: In most of the places you encounter these creatures, they are harmless.

Most are not venomous, you have never suffered any harm from them, they are comparatively microscopic, and you could easily crush them with no effort. The fear of snakes and insects seems irrational, but that does not make it any less real. Remember that with NLP, the issue is not why the fear developed but how to get rid of it.

For this example, look at a fear of spiders. To help you conquer your fear, an NLP practitioner might use something called dissociation. Dissociation means disconnecting from your normal consciousness, as might happen when experiencing or viewing an event from outside of your body. With dissociation, you experience the event as an observer.

In such an example, someone with a fear of spiders would watch him or herself, as if in a movie, encountering spiders. The client would dissociate by imagining floating above, watching him or herself watching a movie where he or she encounters spiders. As in the first example, the therapist may ask the client to include some theme music that does not at all seem to match what is happening in the movie. Using mismatched music for a frightening experience can help the client become desensitized to the difficult experience.

When he or she feels safe to do so, the client can enter into the movie where the phobic encounter has occurred and experience the event in reverse, running it through from end to beginning as quickly as possible. After watching the movie just a few times, the client will begin to notice that his or her feelings have changed from intense fear to moderate, mild, or no fear. It is recommended that the exercise be repeated until the fear is eliminated or feels manageable.

Eye movement desensitization and reprocessing

Eye movement desensitization and reprocessing (EMDR) is a brief therapy method for healing trauma and other emotional issues. You can also use this tool to help you adopt new, more useful behaviors. EMDR uses strategies, such as touch, sound, and eye movements, to engage opposite sides of the brain, encouraging release of difficult emotional experiences. Although EMDR is not commonly used in NLP, it can be an excellent strategy for shifting a state.

EMDR treatment is conducted over eight phases so you will not have an expectation of relief after one visit with a therapist. EMDR has shown to be particularly successful with reprocessing extremely traumatic experiences, such as military combat and sexual assault.

Reprocessing

Reprocessing helps you become less reactive by turning a badly coded experience into one with good coding. You can tell yourself a different story about even the most difficult experiences. You can then store the experience differently in your mind, thus reclaiming power over painful memories. Everything you experience is coded or given meaning and stored in memory. This meaning or code forms the basis of your values, beliefs, and perspective or worldview.

Some memories, particularly difficult or vivid ones, are badly coded. Bad code also becomes part of your belief system. Long-held beliefs, whether based on good code or bad code, are rarely challenged; they feel like second nature or a part of who you are and the reason for what you do. Reprocessing is a powerful tool for behavior modification.

As has been mentioned previously, behavior modification starts not with action but with thought. Many people have experienced thoughts or thought patterns that sabotage their good efforts. It is difficult, especially if your inner critic is bossy and loud, to focus on anything other than that voice. The following exercise helps you quiet the critic so you can hear thoughts that support you in taking action for change.

Reprocessing: An Example

According to the National Public Radio news show *All Things Considered*, fear of clowns, or coulrophobia, is among the top three phobias in Britain. Surprisingly, the other two phobias involve spiders and needles — not flying.

A June 17, 2010 interview on the show with Paul Carpenter of John Lawson's Circus in the U.K., who performs as Popol the clown, tells of his work to help people eliminate their fear of clowns. The sessions, called clownseling, help those with the phobia reprocess by changing what they think and believe about clowns. Participants come into the circus before the crowds and noise and before the clowns get into costume. They have the opportunity to watch the transformation as performers put on their makeup and costumes.

If all goes well, participants can even don their own clown costume and makeup. These clownseling sessions help those with coulrophobia tell themselves a new story about clowns, thus giving them the ability to recode their beliefs and change their behavior on encountering clowns.

EXERCISE 3: HOW TO ADDRESS YOUR INNER CRITIC

The following six steps can help you gain the support of the inner voice that says, "I can't," so you can devote all your resources to discovering how you can. Have your journal on hand for this one; you will need it.

Step 1: Hear the inner voice in clear detail, including the tone, pitch, and words. Is it a voice you recognize? Maybe the voice is repeating negative thoughts or criticisms someone in your life has leveled against you.

Step 2: Ask the critical voice to share the positive intention it is trying to achieve with its criticism. You may need to continue questioning until you find agreement with the positive intention. Maybe the positive intention is to protect you from failure. Remind yourself and the voice: There is no failure, only feedback. Ask until the positive intention is clear.

Step 3: Thank the critical voice for sharing the positive intention. Yes, you read that right: Thank the critical voice. You want to begin to notice and manage your feelings, where before you may have fought with and rejected them.

Step 4: Ask if your inner critic is open to exploring any other possibilities for achieving the positive intention. The answer may not be immediately clear. Being willing to consider the question will help you to stop feeling stuck.

Step 5: Enlist the support of the voice in discovering other possibilities. Choose several of the best possibilities that calm the voice. You do not have to make a decision at this point. You are simply considering your options, and when you remember that the map is not the territory, you know that your options — like you — are unlimited.

Step 6: See yourself vividly experiencing each of the best outcomes. Base your final choice on the outcomes that feel most "right" or comfortable. You should not have a nagging feeling. If you feel any doubt or resistance in any part of your body, pay attention. This likely means you do not have cooperation from your subconscious mind. If the subconscious mind says "no," the plan will not go forward successfully.

NLP helps you address any emotions, thoughts, or beliefs in your personal lives that are not useful. When a belief is not useful, it holds you back and keeps you stuck in places that feel uncomfortable and stifling. These are the places where you are most likely to feel the burden of unrealized potential. That is the pain of not being able to move past thoughts of "If only..." to small and large achievements. NLP helps with creating useful beliefs so you can move, without limits, in any direction.

The benefits of NLP strategies extend to every setting because they deal with the universality of human experiences, including how you think, relate, and communicate; how memories get stored; how beliefs and values are formed; and how information is filtered. NLP is concerned with the structure — individually and collectively — of human experience. Because humans are what you will find in schools, corporations, and homes, NLP is an essential addition to each of these settings.

The Value of NLP in Professional Settings

Watch any commercial or listen to any motivational speaker, and you are likely to recognize many of the principles of NLP because the foundations of NLP, such as language patterns, embedded commands, and presuppositions that people are likely to respond to, are commonly used in each of these arenas.

Do you recognize any of these examples? "I know you are the kind of person who cares about the environment." This statement creates connection by making a positive assumption about the reader — one the reader is not likely to deny or refute. As you hear the statement, you are likely to say to yourself, "Yes, I do care about the environment." When you read this statement, you are likely to feel that whoever made it understands something about you. Again, you begin to feel some connection.

How about this example: "Each of us has the ability to make a difference for our environment." This statement expresses confidence in the reader's ability to take the desired action. The first statement coupled with the second sets up an "if-then" reaction in the listener's thoughts. For example, "If I care about the environment, then I will do something, preferably what the advertiser is asking, to make a difference for the environment." In telling you that they share your environmental concerns, the advertiser has influenced you to take a desired action. In the world of advertisement, the goal is to motivate you to take some action based on your own agreement with the stated premise. For example, you care about the environment so you are likely to be motivated to demonstrate that concern by purchasing a certain brand of car or recycled paper towel.

Much of human interaction is about creating influence. Human beings want to connect and enjoy positive interactions; they need only a little encouragement to do this thing that comes quite naturally. NLP provides that encouragement.

NLP can be used not just in convincing another to take a desired action. It can also be useful in professional settings for things like team building and conflict resolution. Conflict is a normal part of human interaction. In fact, when handled appropriately, it can lead to greater understanding and connection. How can NLP help you manage conflicts appropriately? Try one or all of the following steps for building rapport — yes, you can work to build rapport even in the midst of a conflict — the next time you are at an impasse with a client or co-worker.

- Instead of trying to enforce your point, try to understand what the other person is saying.

- When you think you have an idea about what the person is trying to communicate, backtrack to check for accuracy. This involves repeating what he or she said to you as clearly as possible. For example, say, "Let me be sure I understand," or "It sounds like you are saying."

- Use your voice and body to convey you are listening and you understand. Remember, it does not mean you agree if you understand what a person is trying to say. You can use your voice and body by saying things like, "I understand" or nodding and giving relaxed eye contact while you listen.

- Listen without speaking as the person clarifies his or her point. Conflict is often the result of miscommunication.

- Listen for shared values. Perhaps you have the same goals for the project even though you do not agree on the approach. Use the place of agreement from which to build rapport and connection.

- Listen for the primary representational system (PRS), the dominant sense used in processing information, of the speaker. When you determine what it is, respond with matching words. For example, use responses like "sounds like" for auditory people or "picture this" for visual people.

Building rapport is simply about making connections by showing how you are similar to and understanding of the other person. One of the most important benefits of rapport is it encourages people, even during difficult conversations, to be more agreeable. The benefits are immeasurable.

For example, according to Steve Andreas and Charles Faulkner, NLP experts and authors, 83 percent of all sales are based upon the customer liking the salesperson. When you think about it, just about everyone is in sales. They want people to buy their ideas, act on their instructions, offer them employment, or say yes to a second date.

Consider the following examples.

Jack and Steve are working on a presentation they must complete in one week. They have never worked together and are having a difficult time finding common ground. Each feels confident in his own approach and is unwilling to consider the approach of the other. Steve told his wife after the third day that he and Jack were like oil and water. He could not imagine how they would ever get along. Using an NLP strategy, Jack could decide to be a curious listener rather than an immovable listener as he normally was. He might notice the excited way that Steve described his approach using phrases like, "I feel certain" and "My gut tells me." If Jack knew about NLP, he would also know that those phrases suggest Steve has a kinesthetic representational system. The kinesthetic representational system responds to feelings, including tactile or touch and emotions or feelings. Jack now has a better idea of how to talk with Steve so they can begin to build rapport and arrive at a compromise on their project.

Brenda is responsible for supervising an employee who has underperformed. She has scheduled a meeting with the employee to gain an understanding about what is causing the problem and to consider some performance-improving strategies. Before the meeting begins, Brenda has a clear idea about what she wants to accomplish during the meeting: She wants to hear how the employee views his performance and share her observations. Brenda also wants to understand the best way to motivate the employee; for example, whether he is more likely to move toward incentives or away from disincentives. Brenda will also set clear performance goals with the employee so he can monitor and measure his own progress going forward.

Lastly, Tom has a great idea for a new company project. He wants every employee to be as excited about the project as he is. Because Tom understands that people respond to and frame information differently, he will describe the project using language for each representational system. Tom will help employees see, feel, and hear the benefits of the project. He will also listen to and watch for feedback as he describes the project to each group of employees. He will tailor his delivery to each audience, adopting the listener's point of view as he speaks.

In each of the previous examples, NLP strategies gave professionals an additional tool they could use to address common work issues. Having additional problem solving tools in today's dynamic work environment is important for professionals of all levels. The value of applying NLP strategies is in the flexibility they offer for a variety of situations.

NLP for business communication

NLP helps you become more self-aware. What difference does being self-aware make? It makes a pretty big one, actually. Self-awareness is what you have when you notice how you impact others and how people respond to you. Self-awareness is also about being in tune with yourself, knowing if your current state is most useful, knowing what emotional resources you need for a given situation, and understanding how things going on around you impact you.

Many people without self-awareness in business often seem insensitive. Perhaps they are forceful but not responsive; they do not notice things like morale, cooperation, creativity, or productivity breaking down around them. In fact, many managers often fail to realize how much they rely on stoking fear in employees rather than building rapport with them. Instead, managers would do well to place less emphasis on evaluating performance and more on establishing chemistry and connection. Employees are more likely to perform better and remain in jobs longer when they feel liked and appreciated. Chemistry, another word for rapport, is important for making *all* employees good ones with outstanding performance. Self-awareness is important for creating rapport.

NLP improves self-awareness and self-confidence so that even when faced with difficult situations or just managing a learning curve, business professionals are more likely to achieve success.

NLP provides the tools needed to connect conscious and unconscious resources, thus accessing untapped potential. An example of conscious resources would be training. Resilience and tolerance for setbacks are examples of subconscious resources. Taken together, training and resilience could mean more career opportunities. Also, by creating rapport, you encourage others to invest in your success. When it comes to business, planning, talent, and strategy do matter, but they are amplified by the ability to maintain positive relationships with self and with others.

Consider the following example.

Brenda dreads company parties; she finds them boring. If she used the NLP strategies for creating rapport, she could have more interesting conversations. When rapport is established, conversations that might otherwise seem awkward or halting just flow. If Brenda approaches the conversation with friendly curiosity, she might hear clues about what the speaker values. Brenda could then use these cues to respond to the listener, thus creating feelings of connection and understanding. Because the speaker believes Brenda understands him or her, the speaker will likely share more than small talk.

NLP is a technique for influencing others

NLP is not just for use by secret advertisers; it is a tool of all strong communicators. Using NLP allows you to influence others — hopefully, with integrity. The goal of NLP is not to be manipulative. Rather, it is to understand what appeals to the person you work with. It is to recognize what he or she values because when you know what he or she values, you can adapt your behavior and responses accordingly. This adaptation is the basis of rapport. You can use rapport to connect with clients and co-workers to better understand what they need and want.

For example, Susan is planning a business proposal. She has identified what she thinks will be the most important benefit for her client: increased revenue. The entire proposal is written to highlight this benefit. What Susan does not realize is the client is most interested in creating community goodwill. Consequently, although Susan has created a strong proposal, she is not likely to seal the deal because her proposal does not address the needs and wants of her client at this time. Although it is often brief, there is a relationship between the buyer and seller. Both parties must be considered in what should be viewed as an exchange rather than a one-sided proposition.

Create strong partnerships with NLP

Again, the basis of strong partnerships is rapport. In many cases, individuals must feel some kind of draw or connection to a person before they can begin to feel comfortable with business connections. Though it is true that partnerships form when there is a like for or comfort with the product and dislike of the person, it is also true that partnerships with a like for or rapport with the person and the product have an advantage. When that kind of business magic happens, the connection acts like a catalyst for creativity that streamlines the path to profits and success. If you are not sure how important rapport is for creating strong partnerships, just consider how many business deals happen over coffee, dinner, or a round of golf. Generally speaking, not many people are interested in sharing dinner or an afternoon of golf with someone with which they share no rapport.

Increase productivity with NLP

NLP can increase productivity because it supports clear communication. When you are clear about what you want and how best to communicate that to the listener, the opportunities for miscommunication and wasted efforts reduce. How are productivity and communication related?

- Communication makes it easy to spot knowledge gaps. The bottom line is people perform better when they have a full understanding of the work in which they are tasked; better performance equals higher productivity. For example, does the team member understand how his or her task fits into the larger company function? Can the team member describe his or her responsibilities?

- Communication also helps you understand how people learn. NLP helps you speak the unique language of the person you talk to, which improves learning. People with confidence in their ability to learn a task are more likely to pick up the task and even adapt their skills for better efficiency. For example, when teaching someone to complete a new task or giving directions, it is helpful to know whether they will respond better if you show him or her rather than tell him or her what to do.

- Communication helps build teams that are more resourceful and supportive, thus creating win-win scenarios. In a win-win scenario, everyone feels at least something he or she values or thinks of as important has been addressed. When people feel heard, acknowledged, and included, they are more motivated to perform at their best level. The opposite of this principle was illustrated in June 2010 when Miramar, Florida-based Spirit Airlines canceled several flights, stranding passengers. Why? Because communications between the airline and the pilot's union failed to result in a win-win solution on pay.

Use NLP to Align Values Around Success

Recall the presupposition that "There is no failure, only feedback," as it is particularly useful here. Unintended consequences or poor outcomes can happen in any business situation, but these events are not really the point. More important is what you take away from the experience, how you talked to yourself about the experience, and how you decided to use lessons you took away from that experience. Using the Spirit Airlines example from before, negotiators on both sides should be mindful of this presupposition and review everything that was said and done up to the point of breakdown in communications. They could use information from early negotiations to develop a more successful approach for future talks.

Improve negotiation skills with NLP

Using NLP, skills like rapport building and motivation direction improve negotiation skills by deepening your understanding of what motivates the person with whom you are negotiating. Again, NLP encourages awareness of self and of others so while you talk, it is not just your own interests or ego driving the conversation; it is also your responses to the cues, both verbal and nonverbal, being offered by the person with whom you are negotiating. During the exchange, you are watching, listening, and learning. You are constantly fine tuning your pitch based on what you hear because the goal is to learn what would feel like a win for the listener and to find a way to deliver that win.

You can also improve your negotiation skills by building trust and rapport. Trust is more easily and quickly established by understanding a person's primary, or preferred, representational system (PRS) and responding to it.

The PRS is the most prominent or developed sensory mode used to experience and understand information. The most commonly used senses for interpreting information are visual, auditory, and kinesthetic; gustatory (taste) and olfactory (smell) are also sense modes. A person with a visual representational system uses pictures and images to represent ideas and memories in the brain. Similarly, someone using a kinesthetic representational system calls up the sensations or emotions associated with an experience. Responding to one's primary sense modality helps him or her feel understood *and* helps him or her understand you better because you are using language that represents how he or she thinks about things. Understanding PRS is a powerful tool for influencing others.

EXERCISE 4:
HOW TO DETERMINE
THE PRS BEING USED

There are some general eye cues that can help to identify the primary representational system being used. Use these observations to understand how an individual represents ideas or experiences in his or her mind. When you understand how a person represents ideas, you can improve your chances of building rapport by using the primary representational system during communication. Using words that acknowledge and contribute to the representation sends a signal to the other person that you understand them. That signal facilitates the process of building connection or rapport. The follow observations can be used:

Step 1: When eyes are straight ahead, closed, or move upward and to the left or right, the individual is having visual images in response to the stimulus.

What is happening: The individual is recalling or creating pictures or images in response to the stimulus. Use this information by choosing words that sharpen or clarify the image; choose words that describe the picture or help the individual visualize the experience. For example, if selling a beach vacation to a visual person, describe things like the beauty of the sun or the deep blue of the water.

Step 2: When eyes are level and move to either side or down and to the left, the individual is experiencing auditory images in response to the stimulus.

What is happening: The individual is recalling or creating sounds in response to the stimulus. Use this information by choosing words that bring the sounds to life for the individual. For example, if selling a beach vacation to an auditory person, describe things like the call of the seagulls, the crashing of the waves, or the sound of children laughing.

Step 3: When eyes are down and to the right, the individual is experiencing kinesthetic sensations in response to the stimulus.

What is happening: The individual is recalling emotions or feelings in response to the stimulus. Use this information by choosing words that create sensations for the individual. For example, if selling a beach vacation to a kinesthetic person, describe the feel of the warm sun on skin, the cool water, or the joy of family time.

Responding to the PRS during communication is much like speaking the unique language of the other person. Much like different regions of the country have different dialects and expressions that are unique, individual people respond differently to words and images. Listen and watch when talking to be sure your words evoke the desired response. If not, try to notice the PRS. If you do not remember how to do this, it is all right to fish around a bit. Try using language from each sense mode, and notice the responses. When it looks like you get the best response, you have likely found the best words to use in the conversation. *Chapter 5 will discuss eye-accessing cues as they relate to communication.*

Tools for Creating Rapport

Adopting a communication style that acknowledges the primary representational system of the other person is just one way of building rapport. Other ways of building rapport include matching and mirroring.

Matching

Matching, or making a similar copy of the behavior you see, sets off a pattern of recognition in the person you are talking with, thus making you feel familiar. You can match by adopting the same angle of the head or position of the arms and legs. *A discussion of this technique is included in Chapter 3.*

Mirroring

In this strategy, you provide a mirror image of the behavior you see. Both mirroring and matching increase your comfort level with diverse groups of people, as well as the level of comfort they feel with you.

Matching and mirroring should be subtle enough that you are in sync without being silly. Avoid copying behavior movement by movement. Adopt similar positions using gradual, natural movements. Use behavior similar enough to the behavior you see so it sends a signal to the subconscious mind of the other person that you are somehow the same or like them in some way. People feel more trusting and open with people they perceive as familiar or more like them than different.

Pacing for Rapport

As you no doubt understand by now, the most fundamental aspect of all successful communication is rapport, which you can also develop with pacing. In NLP, pacing is much the same as acknowledging the person you are managing, teaching, or interacting with. You must step into a person's shoes or enter into his or her reality to determine the best approach for giving directions or sharing information. In NLP, stepping into the shoes of another is called the second perceptual position. The first perceptual position is your own viewpoint. From the first position, you consider your own voice, thoughts, and feelings. The second perceptual position lets you step out of your own position to see how a situation looks and feels to the other person. This is the best vantage point from which to imagine how he or she is interpreting what is happening and what he or she is thinking. Successful pacing lays the groundwork for successful leading.

Your success — both personally and professionally — will depend in large measure on your ability to influence others. Be mindful that influencing is not at all synonymous with manipulating. Pacing lays the groundwork for mutual influence. You can accomplish pacing with language, as well as with matching behavior. The following will focus on pacing with language.

Verbal pacing uses information the listener has accepted or knows to be true to lead him or her to accept information not yet known to be true. During pacing, the listener becomes accustomed to agreeing with the speaker because the speaker starts with several true statements. This does not mean there is any dishonesty involved with pacing. It does mean that the listener has not yet accepted what is not yet known to be true as truth. The following is an example of pacing with language:

- **Pace:** You have attended each of the training sessions. This is true; the listener accepts this fact.

- **Pace:** You have read all of the materials. This is true; the listener accepts this as fact.

- **Pace:** You have completed the first phase of the training successfully. This is true; the listener accepts this as fact.

- **Lead:** And now you are ready to begin using what you have learned to meet productivity goals. This is not yet known to be true, but the listener accepts it because he or she is lead to do so based on agreement with previous facts.

Good managers understand the importance of learning the technical aspects of a job and the human or people part, too. Begin by pacing yourself. Use what you know to be true about yourself as the basis for adopting a new skill or behavior. What are your strengths? When are you at your best? Use words to describe where you are and where you want to be. Use what you discover to pace or encourage and lead yourself to the new behavior. Use the following construction to do this: I have been with the company five years — this is true about me (pace); I have had five positive performance reviews — this is also true about me (pace); I have successfully trained two new co-workers, and this is true about me, as well (pace); I am ready to apply for a position on the management team so this can also be true about me (lead). Pacing and leading build confidence by acknowledging accomplishments and using them as a catalyst for future accomplishments or actions. It is impossible to positively motivate people unless you know what is important to them. For example, some people want praise or flexible work schedules as much as or even more than higher pay. NLP helps you determine what is important by learning how to listen and interpret what is communicated. NLP can also help clarify what is important to you with tools that remove non-useful behaviors and that limit thoughts so you can pursue your goals with singular focus.

For example, if your goal is to increase your own productivity by 5 percent, a non-useful behavior might be putting off undesirable tasks. The behavior is at odds with the goal. An example of limiting thoughts in this instance includes thoughts like, "I will never be able to focus on these reports" or "I will never be able to deal with difficult customers confidently." You could change your limiting thoughts and increase your confidence by using the Swish pattern. The Swish pattern is a quick and easy tool for replacing non-useful thoughts and behaviors with useful ones.

The Swish Pattern

Begin by taking a few moments to identify any thoughts, feelings, or images that accompany the non-useful or limiting thought.

Decide on an image you can use instead of the one currently associated with the limiting thoughts. For example, if each time you have the non-useful thought you automatically see yourself cowering or looking nervous, instead, picture yourself standing straight and looking confident. Experience this positive picture vividly, as if watching a movie.

Adopting the first perceptual position, try to understand what ordinarily triggers the negative picture. Do you notice a pattern of thoughts or feelings?

Bring the images together. Imagine using the picture-in-picture feature on a television set. The positive image is a small image in the corner of the larger negative image. Just as you would with your remote control, quickly switch the images in the screen of your mind. The positive image will now be the larger image.

Once you have established good pacing, you can begin to lead. Leading is much like influencing. Here, you must help people develop thoughts that are in line with organizational goals and lead to actions that meet those goals. Motivating people to take action first requires getting them in a "yes" mood or pacing them. Pacing sets up an energized path on which to lead or sweep employees along in a particular direction. Without pacing, managers may find employees setting out in the wrong direction or perhaps unmotivated to move in any direction at all. These ideas are not just for managers because, again, everyone manages people in a sense, and everyone sells something, whether it is his or her next big idea or him or herself on an interview or a date.

How else can NLP help you at work?

NLP helps employees provide better customer service by using pacing behavior. For example, manage angry customers by matching or adopting some of their behaviors to create rapport. You will want to express the same urgency and energy you hear in the voice of the customer expressing a problem. The customer should feel that you share the same concern over the problem at hand. When you respond, you should have a similar but not identical — perhaps even a shade lower than the customer's volume and speed. Think of voice matching as falling in step with someone as you walk side by side. By doing so, you will build rapport because the customer feels that his or her feelings and the problem have been acknowledged. The customer is now likely ready to be led into speaking more calmly. Maintain your patience and calmness during the exchange by remembering the presupposition that "underlying every behavior is a positive intention." Remember that this outburst is not about ruining your day but is instead a non-useful strategy for realizing a positive intent.

Matching is one way of using NLP at work; clarifying meaning is another way. You can use backtracking — or rephrasing what was said — to show understanding and eliminate miscommunication. Using this strategy, you might say something like, "It sounds like you are saying…" or "Let me see if I understand what you are saying..." Not sure how to clarify meaning to improve communication? Remember that NLP is about modeling human excellence. Think of someone who does a good job avoiding miscommunication. Watch what they do. How do they position themselves? What do they say? What tone do they use? What do successful people do in meetings? Study each aspect of his or her behavior. Which aspects would be most useful for you to model? Try it, and note your results. Modify your results accordingly.

Outcome thinking

It is easy, and quite common, to become caught up with the problem or what goes wrong. Unfortunately, this practice is common but not useful. Thinking in terms of outcomes instead provides the focus you need to avoid random tasks that are not useful. When you know what you want, you can tailor what you do to get it. The bottom line is you are always going to get some type of result. Get the one you want by first shaping a well-formed outcome. *Chapter 4 includes a detailed discussion of outcome thinking.*

Outcome thinking helps you readjust your focus so you look for what you want rather than what goes wrong. It is important to be ever mindful of outcome thinking in the workplace because such thinking is instructive. Outcome thinking teaches you to train your thoughts and actions in a planned direction. Here is another way to consider outcome thinking: Imagine being part of a race as an individual or member of a team. This is the only information you have.

You do not know whether you are participating in a 5K, 10K, or even a marathon. Moreover, you have not been told where the finish line is, how many weeks you have to train, or what finishing time you should train for. How would you begin your approach? What will guide your actions?

Now consider this scenario. You are training with your work team to complete a 10K in ten weeks. Because you will compete against another work team, the team captain has set a goal to have your team complete the race with an average time of 60 minutes, about a ten-minute mile. How does knowing the desired outcome — completing a 10K in ten weeks at about ten minutes per mile — impact your thoughts and actions regarding training for the race? Now, imagine your right knee has given you trouble. You are more likely to succeed with your training program if you focus your attention on solutions for your knee rather than the problem. Focusing on the pain in your knee siphons energy you would otherwise use to achieve your outcome. A more useful strategy would focus on a solution. For example, you could visit a specialty running store for advice, make an appointment with a doctor who treats sports injuries, or consult a running coach.

The Value of NLP in Education

Just as in counseling, coaching, or business, teachers can improve their success by valuing relationships with their students. The following is another presupposition of NLP that is especially useful at work, as well as in the classroom: The person who sets the frame controls the communication and the actions that happen. Teachers are, in fact, leaders. They set the tone and the culture of the classroom. Teachers also set expectations for the classroom. Everyone should have a clear understanding of what is expected before they can be successful with what they are being asked to do. This is why communication is so important. It is also important to understand how the people you talk to are deciding what is meant by what you say. For example, "I have to run" could mean someone is in a hurry or imply he or she does not feel right unless he or she gets in a few miles each day. NLP helps you decipher what the person is saying, even with children, by helping you choose language with the listener in mind. In addition to improving communication, NLP can also help teachers improve student behavior and learning, as well as their own performance.

Use NLP to improve the educational experience for teachers and students

The NLP toolbox for teachers is bottomless. Teachers can use it to help with presentation, influencing, building rapport, and self-management. The following are a few of the most effective strategies you can use to begin getting results today:

- **Use behavioral flexibility.** Teaching diverse groups of students requires some flexibility. You cannot adapt to what goes on around you if it looks like you are headed for an undesirable result. Learn to correct your course; it is important to adapt as you go to get to the desired result. Of course, you must be clear about the desired result at the outset. For example, if the lesson you have planned seems difficult for a majority of the students to stay focused on, do you press forward, pause, change your presentation approach, or delay the lesson for another time? Given the pressures teachers face with administrators and testing outcomes, it is a fair bet that many feel there is no choice other than to press on with the lesson. If you must continue the lesson even when students do not seem engaged, remember two important presuppositions presented earlier: "The meaning of communication is the response you get" and "If what you are doing is not working, do something else." Ultimately, teachers cannot control students, but they can control themselves. Adapt your approach until it works to achieve your desired outcome — in this case, student attention.

- **Decide what you want.** Have you defined the desirable result? A goal of improved behavior is vague. Instead, you might say that you want Susan to respond without calling out or Johnny to get permission before leaving his seat. When talking with students, it is important to clearly state what you want in positive terms. For example, rather than saying, "No talking," instead say, "Please work quietly." Students must have a clear idea of what is expected if they are to be successful.

- **Practice sensory awareness.** Do you notice what goes on within and around you? Can you use this information to manage communication? This is particularly important in the classroom. Children respond to more than what you say. They make decisions based on your body language, facial cues, and tone of voice. Be mindful of how you come across. You can check this by watching how the children respond. If you do not get the desired response, remember, you are the leader in this communication exchange; you can change your presentation. For example, a frown might not feel encouraging for students working through tough math problems.

- **Build rapport.** Have you taken a moment to determine if you are thinking useful thoughts? Do you know what your current state is and how it will impact the other pillars? You will recall the four pillars are rapport, outcome thinking, sensory awareness, and behavioral flexibility. Remember, when you are not in a resourceful state, you can trigger an anchor to quickly return to one. Before beginning your day and during each break, decide which state would be the most useful for the next part of your day. Name the state. Do you need to be calm and comforting or silly and light? Use a predetermined anchor to get into your state and watch the quality of your classroom interactions improve dramatically.

Promote positive learning behaviors

NLP is an excellent tool for determining what type of learners your students are. This alone can be very helpful because it creates a win-win situation. Students experience more effective learning, and teachers more effectively teach students. The following is a brief introduction to learning using the primary representational systems (PRS) discussed earlier in the chapter.

Visual learners

Visual learners are normally good spellers. These students retain more of what they see than what they hear and do not find noise to be a distraction. What other qualities have you noticed among visual learners in your classroom? For example, these learners respond well to maps, graphs, charts, and tables. What would be a few good phrases to use when talking with visual learners? You might consider phrases like, "Can you see the difference" or "Visualize South Dakota on the map."

Auditory learners

Auditory learners find noise to be a distraction. They retain more of what they hear rather than what they see. These students are normally better at oral than written tasks. As you might have guessed, they are also talkative. Chances are you have had more than a few auditory learners in your classes. What other patterns have you noticed in their behavior? For example, you might have noticed that auditory learners are easily distracted by noise. What strategies might you use in developing rapport with these students? With younger learners, rhyming games and songs are particularly helpful. Older auditory learners benefit more from oral rather than written instructions and information.

Kinesthetic learners

Kinesthetic learners prefer hands-on learning experiences. They find it difficult to sit still for long periods and want to show you more than they want to tell you. Kinesthetic learners experience feelings and sensations in response to stimulus. What qualities have you noticed among your students? These students love to get their hands on things and appreciate opportunities for movement. Use this information to plan lessons that include building, dissecting, walking, assembling, and other body-involved activities.

Six NLP strategies for the teacher's tool box

The following six strategies can help teachers more effectively manage classrooms and improve student learning. The emphasis with these strategies is on communication and rapport — the building blocks of any successful relationship.

1. **Use language to improve learning.** Understand the importance of language and how individual students will take meaning from what you do and do not say. Language has two levels. The first level of language structure is surface structure — the face value of the words. Here is an example: "Hello, class. I will be filling in until Mr. Jones comes back from his

honeymoon." The unspoken information that can be gleaned from the surface structure is called deep structure — the second level. The deep structure, which is the unspoken or underlying information communicated in the words, leads you to conclude that the teacher, Mr. Jones, has gotten married. Try to anticipate what meaning children will take away from your sentences before you use them.

2. **Achieve agreement in the classroom.** It is a good idea for teachers to present choices so that whichever choice the student makes, the desired outcome is achieved. For example, you could ask the student, "Would you like to start with spelling or reading?" Because the teacher would be happy with either choice, he or she will achieve the desired outcome of getting the student to do reading or spelling regardless of which choice is made. Remember to manage your expectations, as they will be revealed through unconscious communication. Children can recognize resignation or discouragement a mile away so look like you expect a positive outcome when you speak.

3. **Speak with positive assumptions.** Teachers can use positive assumptions to encourage children. For example, saying, "We will learn even more in the next chapter" asserts that the student has already learned a lot. Similarly, telling the student, "The second part is the hardest" assumes the parts following the next part will be easier and

can encourage or inspire confidence, or relief, depending on the child.

4. **Cover your bases.** Foster feelings of inclusion with the NLP strategy of covering all bases. When you cover your bases, you make statements that include every child in the room. No student feels left out, and every student feels like you are talking to or about him or her. For example, tell a class of high school students: "Some of you will go on to college after graduation; others may travel for the summer or look for work." Notice that in this example, everyone is included, thus you cover all the bases. Creating an environment of inclusion fosters feelings of belonging and connection.

5. **Use yes tags to get agreement.** Using yes tags is another strategy teachers can use to gain agreement or cooperation from students. Yes tags are the same as verbal pacing in that they present consecutive facts the student accepts as true followed by a command and a final fact. The more times a student says yes to the accepted facts, the more likely the student will accept the command. Following the command with a final fact increases the likelihood that the command will be accepted as inevitable.

Here is an example of how to use a yes tag: You have prepared all year for standardized testing (yes fact). Testing begins next month (yes fact). You must pass the test to be promoted (yes fact).

This week is a good time to begin working on the practice tests (command), wouldn't it? (Yes, final fact).

6. **Use positive language to improve outcomes.** Use language to help students focus on desired behavior. Using language that highlights behavior you do not want often sets up a subconscious focus on that very behavior. In other words, say what you want rather than what you do not want. For example, instead of commanding, "Do not run," you could say, "Please walk." Because students respond to what they hear, you should avoid words that focus their attention on the action you do not want. Using commands like, "Do not run," causes the listener to focus on the word run rather than the preferred action, which is to walk. Direct your listener to the intended outcome by using language that features that outcome.

You can also use positive language to manage your own behavior in the classroom. Do this by recoding or reframing a bad day. Consider the following example: Joan teaches a combined class of young elementary school students with special needs. Her students range from first-graders to third-graders. Two of the boys are partially toilet trained. Joan has spoken repeatedly to one student's parents about remembering to bring a change of clothes each day. They only remember sometimes, and the pants and underwear Joan brought in herself yesterday have been soiled. The student had another accident today, and Joan is beginning to feel frustrated and not supported. To make matters worse, this student had a big toileting accident, which soiled the floor; two other children tracked the soil on their way to the coat room. What a day for her assistant to be out sick.

Yes, Joan had a really bad day in the classroom. Every teacher experiences a bad classroom day from time to time. What now? It is up to you. You can reframe or recode bad experiences so you do not stay stuck in that unpleasant place. The following is an exercise you can use to recode a bad classroom experience.

EXERCISE 5:
RECODING
BAD EXPERIENCES

Take a moment, and use the following exercise to recode a bad experience. Recoding allows you to identify your current feelings about an experience and change the way you describe and feel about that experience. The shift recoding facilitates is freeing because it means you need not be stuck with bad feelings.

Step 1: Create two columns on a piece of paper. Label one column "How I feel about what happened" and the other column "How I would like to feel about what happened." You will not need to write about what happened, only how you would like to feel about the experience.

Step 2: Write at least three to five feeling words in each column. The following are some examples of feeling words that Joan might use:

How I feel about what happened:

- Angry
- Frustrated
- Not supported

How I would like to feel about what happened:

- Compassionate
- Resourceful
- Supported

Step 3: Breathe deeply. Ask yourself if your current feelings are useful. Ask yourself what you need to change your feelings, and what the benefit of changing your feelings would be. You might need to look for a more useful way to view troubling classroom behavior. For example, an obstinate child could be thought of as tenacious instead — a good candidate for the debate team. You might need to remind yourself about what went right. For example, even though you were dealing with a difficult child, you remained patient. Or, remind yourself that the day went well except for the last hour. You could tell yourself that changing your feelings is important for developing or maintaining satisfaction with your work as a teacher.

In Joan's case, she might remind herself that the student is making progress because unlike last month, the student has had only four accidents; it may just be that he is having a setback this week. Also, Joan might consider that the student's parents do not have a washer, which makes it especially challenging to send him with a change of clothes. Joan fosters her feelings of resourcefulness by purchasing several sets of pants and underwear on 50-percent-off day at the thrift store. She also tweaks her approach so the student receives more frequent positive feedback for avoiding toileting accidents.

Step 4: Focus on how you feel about what happened. See the feelings as light. As you breathe deeply, see the lights begin to dim. Notice any tension in your body as you move through this step.

Step 5: Now, think about how you would like to feel about what happened. Experience the feelings as radiant energy you take in with each breath; the more deeply you breath, the more you take in the good feelings. Continue this process until you feel the way you would like to feel.

Step 6: Return to your written list. Cross out everything in column one and read column two aloud. For example, say to yourself, "I feel resourceful." You might further reinforce this feeling by providing evidence to yourself. Joan might point to her purchase of pants and underwear at a discount to have on hand as evidence of her resourcefulness.

With time, this exercise will become part of an automatic strategy repertoire for managing feelings around bad experiences. NLP gives you the tools to be deliberate about how you choose to respond to everything that happens within and around you. In addition to managing feelings, it is also important to manage motivation. NLP can help you do that, too.

NLP is useful for changing your feelings and also helpful with encouraging feelings, such as desire to complete an unpleasant task. The following exercise will help you take action when you find your motivation waning or just plain missing.

EXERCISE 6:
MOTIVATING YOURSELF
TO TAKE ACTION

Sometimes it seems the to-do list grows in direct proportion to waning motivation to tackle it. Manage yourself in the classroom, as well as in your administrative responsibilities. Try the following exercise to motivate yourself to tackle tasks with enthusiasm instead of half-hearted dread:

The Godiva® Chocolate pattern is named for the intense feelings of desire and pleasure lush chocolate inspires. This technique helps the user transfer or associate positive feelings from an activity that is enjoyed to an activity that is not enjoyed to create motivation for doing it.

Use the Godiva Chocolate pattern to motivate yourself when faced with a task you are dreading.

Step 1: Think of something you are very excited about. It could be something you have done or something you fantasize about doing. See, hear, and feel yourself having this wonderful experience. The image in your mind is called Picture 1.

Step 2: Take a break, and observe your surroundings. The goal here is to break state. Breaking state is simply moving out of the feelings or state of mind that you are experiencing in the moment.

Step 3: Think of the task you dread. See yourself completing the task, or imagine as if you are observing yourself doing the task. This is Picture 2.

Step 4: Check in with yourself to see if Picture 2 is what you really want. It is important to stop and notice how you are feeling at this point. Are there any feelings of objection in your mind or body? In other words, is there any reason you do not want to enjoy the task for which you are trying to create motivation? If so, you will need to work through or reframe your objections before you can move forward. *See the sidebar later in this chapter on reframing for more information.*

Step 5: Place Picture 2, the activity you are not enthusiastic about yet, behind Picture 1 in your mind. Do this by imagining two photographs on a clothing rack. Picture 2 should be positioned behind Picture 1 on the rack.

Step 6: Imagine a connection between the pictures sitting on the clothing rack in your mind. While doing this, create a small hole in Picture 1. It should be just large enough that you can see Picture 2 through the hole.

Step 7: Allow all the images and feelings from Picture 1 to spill through the hole onto Picture 2. Picture 1 will begin to cover Picture 2, and you will begin to transfer the excitement you feel from Picture 1 to Picture 2.

Step 8: Keeping the excitement in place, imagine yourself closing the hole.

Step 9: Repeat as needed until the feelings associated with Picture 1 become completely associated with Picture 2.

How to Effectively Talk to Parents about Problem Behavior

Begin by putting yourself in the parent's shoes or in the second perceptual position. If you were in the parent's position, what information would be important for you to hear and what would be the best way to hear it? Remember to be specific about the problem behavior. For example, when and how frequently does the behavior happen and under what conditions? What behavior would you like to see instead? How can you partner with parents to encourage this behavior? How often will you follow up or provide feedback to the parent and student as behavior improves?

You can also use this exercise to have more successful parent-teacher conferences, particularly when dealing with difficult parents. Use the pattern to associate the conference experience with good feelings. After you drum up enthusiasm for another late night of parent-teacher conferences, maintain your good feelings, or state, with the use of an anchor.

As you may recall, an anchor is an external signal planned to elicit an internal response. For example, if every time you feel calm and centered you fold your hands together, eventually the act of folding your hands would elicit feelings of calmness. In this example, folding the hands together is referred to as "firing the anchor." If the desired result is achieved — feeling calm — you have triggered the state.

Another way to manage problem situations is to set your focus on the outcome you want rather than the problem. This strategy works because your energy goes to the thing you focus on. Use the example of the parent-teacher conference to come up with a few sentences to describe how you want the evening to go. Be intentional about using positive language in your descriptive sentences. "I will enjoy a good conversation with Jim's parents, I will get a good response from parents to my new ideas for the next science module, and I will feel confident and engaged," are all good examples.

Reframing

At any given time, we are faced with so much information that it is impossible to consciously take it all in. Imagine that information is as vast as the sky. The information you consciously take in is said to be within your frame. You put a frame around the portion of sky or information that you consciously take in. Reframing allows you to consider more and/or different information. Imagining the sky again, reframing is much like enlarging, or shifting, the original frame. For example, Alisa has some, but not all, of the money needed for her car payment. She is so consumed with worry that she cannot even consider any options to help the situation. Her thoughts remain only on the money she lacks; they do not turn to options, such as calling the car company to make arrangements, borrowing the money, turning in the car, or even earning extra money. Reframing provides a different perspective from which more possibilities or choices emerge.

Robert Dilts on creating change

Robert Dilts worked with and studied with Bandler and Grinder, the co-creators of NLP. He holds a bachelor's degree in behavioral technology from the University of California at Santa Cruz, the same university where Bandler and Grinder conducted much of the research on which NLP is based. Dilts worked with other NLP contributors, including Milton Erickson and Gregory Bateson. He is the author or co-author of nearly 20 books, such as *Sleight of Mouth: The Magic of Conversational Belief Change* and *Beliefs: Pathways to Health & Well-Being*.

Dilts' contribution to the understanding of how change is created is significant. His logical levels help people understand how they can create change in their own lives, as well as on larger scales, such as within organizations or systems. There are six levels:

1. **Spirit.** What is the larger purpose? Why does what you do matter? Schools may be concerned with educating future leaders. Companies may be concerned with branding or community relations. Individuals may connect work with sense of self or life purpose.

2. **Identity.** Who do you think you are as an organization or individual? Organizations may see themselves as industry leaders. An individual may see him or herself as a competent employee who is valued by the organization and skilled at reaching students.

3. **Beliefs.** What does the individual or company value or believe is true? For example, a company may believe strong customer service and relevant products equal a strong bottom line. A teacher may believe the best way to reach students is to understand their unique learning style.

4. **Capabilities.** How do things get done? What skills or strategies does the company or individual use?

5. **Behaviors.** What behaviors are present?

6. **Environments.** How do external influences impact present behavior?

Consider the following example to learn how the levels might look through the eyes of a teacher.

According to Leigh Williams Steere, co-owner of Managing People Better, LLC, Dilts' concept is this: In order to successfully enact a change, you must work at the level above the area you are trying to change. For example, if you want to change a behavior, then the answer is at a level somewhere above behavior. It might be a capability issue, a belief issue, an identity issue, or a spiritual issue. An environmental change is no more than a temporary fix. Steere goes on to say that most organizations shy away from considering the "spirit" part of Dilts' concept, and many corporate coaches work at the capability level and not higher than that, which is why backsliding among coaching clients is common.

If your goal is to create change in your own life or on an organizational level, begin with an understanding of where the problem lies. For example, if a teacher noticed disruptive behavior, she or he could create change by working on one of the higher levels. His or her thinking might look like this:

- **Behavior:** What behaviors are present? Joshua is disruptive every afternoon. The teacher can look at capabilities. Science is the first class in the afternoon, and Joshua is often bored because he does not read well.

- **Beliefs:** He or she might also look at Joshua's belief that science is for geeks so he is not interested. Because he is not engaged, he is disruptive.

- **Capability:** The teacher could affect change by helping Joshua improve his reading skills or capability so he is not bored and, therefore, less likely to be disruptive.

- **Beliefs:** The teacher can also find someone "cool" who Joshua admires to inspire his interest in science. Again, because Joshua is engaged, he is less likely to be disruptive.

- **Environment:** Joshua might be helped by having his desk moved to the front from the back of the room to eliminate distractions. He might also perform better in a class with fewer students.

If the teacher had simply engaged Joshua on the level of the problem, he or she might have come up with solutions that addressed the underlying cause of his disruptions.

There are a number of challenges and joys with teaching. NLP can help teachers navigate those challenges just by providing the tools to improve communication, maintain the most resourceful emotional state, and reframe information and assumptions. NLP can even help teachers feel more charismatic, confident, and influential — all important qualities for success.

Use NLP in Your Personal Life

The most important uses for NLP in personal life involve improved communication. These tools help you develop a good relationship with yourself, as well as with others. The tools also help eliminate unwanted behaviors and motivating yourself to adopt new habits and skills. At the heart of these changes is belief.

When ready to embark on any change or accomplish any goal, you should understand at least three things: How the goal fits into your individual and larger life systems, what beliefs support your current state, and what beliefs you need to support your desired state. Consider each of these questions as you move through the next section on NLP in personal life.

The Value of NLP in improving relationships

Communication is not just about the way you talk to others; it is also about the way you talk to yourself. NLP provides the tools for building strong communication skills that improve relationships and personal success. One of the best ways to improve communications skills and improve professional and personal relationships is to learn how to build rapport. Rapport is simply creating alignment or connection with another person. When there is no rapport, there is often resistance, misunderstanding, and feelings of not being heard or understood. When you build rapport, you foster feelings of understanding, familiarity, and appreciation — feelings to which most people respond positively.

You can build rapport by using techniques discussed earlier, such as matching and mirroring, which involve adopting the same posture or tone of voice as the person with whom you are interacting. You can also build rapport by adopting his or her point of view during the interaction. Look for clues that can help you determine what he or she is thinking or how he or she is feeling. Clarify for accuracy, and respond positively to what you learn. Finally, you can achieve rapport by letting your behavior reflect the state you want others to feel about you. For example, do you want others to experience you as compassionate, confident, concerned or angry, anxious, and self-centered?

Release phobias and painful memories

Releasing fears or painful memories is not simply a matter of showing your thoughts who is boss; it is about changing the feelings associated with the thoughts. NLP is effective for releasing painful memories or overcoming fears using association and dissociation. Association is experiencing or seeing the world through your own body. Dissociation is experiencing or seeing the world from outside of your own body or as an observer. NLP tools take the pain away from difficult memories by helping individuals learn to dissociate painful feelings from the bad experience and associate the experience with neutral feelings.

To dissociate from phobias or painful memories, see yourself experiencing the difficult memory on a screen or in a picture. See the picture as an interested observer — dissociated from it — rather than as the person having the experience — associated with it. Imagine the picture or screen moving farther away, becoming blurry and less clear. As the picture fades, verbally release the feeling. For example, think to yourself, "I release any feelings of anger." As you release the unwanted feelings, verbally invite wanted feelings by telling yourself, "I choose to feel peaceful." Try the exercise with several different unwanted feelings. You will find that when you separate the feeling from the experience, you eliminate painful feelings.

Decrease stress and anxiety

Relieving stress and anxiety is about more than thinking calm and peaceful thoughts. "Mapping across," an important tool developed by NLP founders Bandler and Grinder, is useful for decreasing anxiety and stress. Mapping across allows you to transfer an identity or skill from one situation to another. In other words, mapping across helps you take useful resources from one state into another. For example, suppose Susan is great with customers at work, even difficult ones. She can establish rapport, she can pace when customers shout angrily, and she can lead them into calmer states. At home, Susan cannot seem to have a civil conversation with her teenage daughter. Mapping across allows Susan to identify the strong people skills she has in one setting and enlist them to improve communication in the setting where she has trouble. The goal here is for Susan to bring her identity as a competent communicator into interactions with her daughter. Susan can do this by triggering the state she uses at work in interactions with her daughter. Susan must first establish an anchor that is associated with the state she is in when communicating well. For example, each time she is calm and resourceful as she calms an angry customer at work, Susan places her hand on her shoulder. With time, the action will become associated with the state. Susan can use that action to trigger the state she will need to communicate effectively with her daughter.

Eliminate unwanted behaviors

It takes more than willpower to eliminate unwanted behaviors, such as overeating or smoking. People want to make important changes in their lives that help them feel better, achieve more success, and enjoy deeper connections with the people they care about. That people often fail in making these changes is not a matter of wanting something impossible or unattainable; it is a matter of approach.

When it comes to making life changes, our efforts must focus on strategies such as aligning, associating, and visualizing rather than wishing, agonizing, and struggling. Creating change of any type is absolutely possible when you begin from within. Think about something that you have tried to change in the past. Perhaps you wanted to quit smoking. Remember making the decision and even writing it or saying it aloud. Think about how you felt and what you were thinking as you made the decision. If you were not able to eliminate the habit, chances are that in addition to the excitement or hopefulness you felt about being smoke-free, you also felt fear, doubt, or anxiety.

Doing something different requires congruence. With congruence, all of your thoughts, goals, and behaviors are in agreement. We will review the example of smoking to demonstrate. The goal was to stop smoking, but the behavior, which may have included cravings and feelings of irritability, did not support the goal. Also, your thoughts, which may have sounded like, "This is harder than I thought," "I do not know how else to handle my stress," and "It is not fair to my friends or family that I am so irritable," did not support the goal. Given that the thoughts, behavior, and goal about quitting smoking were at odds or incongruent, it is unlikely that the goal will be accomplished.

The best way to accomplish your goals is to be sure that you start with a goal that can be accomplished. Goals must take a number of factors into consideration. In other words, goals must be intentional, well thought out, or well formed.

How to design a well-formed goal

Start by being very clear about what you want. Use positive language to state what you want. For example, instead of saying, "I do not want to be a smoker anymore," say, "I want to be smoke-free." Phrasing is important here because it shifts the focus from what you do not want to what you do want. NLP has come up with six things to consider when designing a goal with the best chance for success. Use the following list when developing your own goals:

1. **Determine if what you want is fully within your control.** If any portion of your goal requires change or action from someone other than you, you cannot be fully in control of the outcome. Your goal should also be possible for you. For example, though it may be possible to improve your golf score, it may not be possible to compete with Tiger Woods at the Masters.

2. **Decide how you will know when your goal has been accomplished.** For example, suppose your goal is to become a better parent. How will you know when you have accomplished your goal? You are more likely to have evidence of success if your goals are measurable. An example of how you might measure your success of becoming a better parent include:

   • I will know I have accomplished my goal of becoming a better parent:

> o When I have helped my children with homework each night.
> o When I give my child ten minutes of my undivided attention at least three times each week.
> o When I have completed a parenting class.
> o When I handle my frustration without yelling.
> o When I teach my child something new.
> o When I let my child lead an activity instead of always telling him or her what we are going to do.

3. **Review the larger impact of your goal to determine if the goal fits into your life as it is at this time.** In other words, look at the whole of your life and the important people in it. How and what will be affected as you work toward your goal? What fallout or obstacles do you anticipate? Planning ahead can help you successfully navigate those obstacles, thus improving your chances for success.

4. **Create a compelling future.** See yourself moving along the path toward your goal. Imagine where you are right now, and see yourself moving until you get to where you want to go. Once there, give yourself over to the experience of the achievement. Allow yourself to revel in the sights, sounds, tastes, smells, words, colors, and weather. Use all of your senses to fully enter into the experience of the achievement.

5. **Develop your plan.** Now that you have your plan in place, it is time to fast forward to the feeling of accomplishment. Pretending the goal has already been accomplished makes it feel more real. Use the following steps to anticipate the success feelings that will come with meeting your goal:

   • **Visit your goal.** Vividly experience the joy and pride of achieving your goal.

   • **See your future.** Notice how achieving your goal has improved your life.

   • **See your past.** Retrace the path you took to get to your future. Notice how the journey has changed you.

   • **Walk back along your path.** Recall what you did to achieve your goal. Remember the support you had and how you encouraged yourself.

   • **Notice the steps along your path.** Recall the resources and abilities you marshaled to achieve your goal, the order of steps you used, and the time it took.

   • **Focus on now.** You should have a full appreciation of what it will take to reach your goal and how it will feel to achieve your goal.

6. **Run through a dress rehearsal.** Most significant accomplishments happen at least twice: once in

the mind and again in reality. The first time you accomplish the goal is a dress rehearsal of sorts. The dress rehearsal provides confidence that you can achieve success. The dress rehearsal also provides another opportunity to experience the feelings of success associated with meeting a goal. Use the following steps to imagine you have already met your goal:

- **Assume the role.** Use the language, thoughts, and postures associated with your new role.

- **Walk the path.** Trace the path that led you to your goal. See yourself at the end of the path looking back to the beginning.

- **"Beam" yourself back.** Retrace your steps on the path so you are back at the beginning. See the steps in front of you as doable.

Take action

Accomplishing a goal requires planning for accountability. Being accountable helps you set important time limits and establish a list of tasks you can check off as you make progress toward your goal. The following are the steps to take in creating your plan for accountability:

- **Make a date.** I will begin working on my goal on Jan. 1. I will complete my goal by June 1.

- **Establish benchmarks.** Break your goal into steps you can accomplish in the short term. For example: "I will find an exercise partner by June 15 or week one," and "I will have lost four pounds by month one or July 15." Mark your calendar or PDA, or write and post your dates where you can see them.

- **Stay focused on your vision.** See yourself at various stages along the path to goal completion, visualize yourself completing your goal, and imagine what you will look like and how you will feel after you accomplish your goal. Remember to engage all of your senses in the experience so it feels as if you have achieved the goal before you accomplish it.

- **Get started.** Even the best plan is meaningless unless it is paired with action. You must start your plan and work through it step by step to complete it successfully.

Perceptual positions

Perceptual positions are like viewpoints or places from which you interpret information. Different positions provide different views or perspectives about what is happening and how it is understood. Perceptual positions help you with visualization and are critical for association and dissociation. There are five positions:

- **First position:** This is the associated position. From here, you fully experience what happens in your own body and through your own eyes. You allow yourself to feel, see, and hear what goes on and use that information to stand grounded in your inner power.

- **Second position:** This position gives you the perspective of the person you communicate with. From here, you try to imagine how you sound, look, and feel to the person you interact with. You step into that person's shoes to gain insight into how he or she experiences you.

- **Third position:** This is the dissociated position. This position allows you to be objective or detached from emotions, particularly difficult ones. Assuming this position is almost like watching a movie — you observe rather than participate.

- **Fourth position:** This position provides an overview perspective. From here, you are concerned with understanding what goes on with all of the participants and the system that connects them.

- **Fifth position:** This is the cosmic view or transcendent view. This position is most easily achieved through meditation.

You can use perceptual positions to improve confidence, reduce anxiety, or create your desired state.

Work to align your perceptual positions. For example, when in first position, you should not project your thoughts or feelings on to the second position. This is often how miscommunication occurs; you decide how another person feels or what he or she thinks instead of letting that person communicate his or her own feelings. What you should hear from second position is what that person thinks and feels and not what you think or feel. No, NLP does not give you the power to read minds. It does help you become attuned to clues about what a person might think or feel based on body language and word choice. If you are uncertain about how to interpret what you see or hear, do not be afraid to clarify with the speaker. The following is a basic example. Suppose you are talking with someone who briskly runs his or her hands along his or her arms. If you are not sure whether he or she has a sudden case of goose bumps or is simply chilly, you can ask. Likewise, if you give an afternoon talk and a participant yawns, it would be inappropriate to immediately conclude he or she yawned because your presentation is boring. He or she might have yawned because your workshop falls just after the conference luncheon or even because of medication. Aligning perceptual positions allows you to look for clues rather than arrive at false conclusions. An important key for communication is understanding the position of the other. It is impossible to understand the position of the other if you are unwilling to look beyond your own position.

Use NLP to improve self-image

Poor self-image requires changing your internal representation, or the way you think of yourself. Your thoughts create your reality. To move past your own mental limitations, you must change your mind.

Many of the presuppositions of NLP are designed to help individuals use strength-based explanations when examining their behaviors. These positive ways of talking about yourself remind you that even if you have made mistakes, you are still capable of achieving success. For example, if you subscribe to the ideas that people are not broken, they work perfectly, and every behavior has a positive intent:

• You can acknowledge your innate perfection.

• You can immediately stop beating yourself up.

• You can instead start looking for useful behavior to replace the dysfunctional behavior you previously used to get at your intent.

If you know you are more than your behavior:

• You know that who you are — lovable, complete, and worthy, for example — is not at all related to what you do.

If you know there is no failure, only feedback:

• You can look for the lessons hidden in what you previously called failures.

- You can use that feedback to find new strategies to get you what you want.

- You can begin to see yourself as someone in process of accomplishing a goal or building a skill rather than as a failure.

Much like you can visualize yourself meeting other goals, such as improving your performance, you can visualize yourself feeling like you want to feel about yourself. Step into the experience of accomplishing your goal as if it is happening.

Another strategy for building self-esteem is to imagine how someone who really loves you or who has deep appreciation for you feels about you. Add those feelings and thoughts to your beliefs about yourself.

The Circle of Excellence pattern

One way to develop more esteem and appreciation for yourself is to practice the Circle of Excellence pattern. This pattern helps you harness inner resources, such as confidence, so you can apply them whenever the need arises. You can use the Circle of Excellence pattern to move out of negative states. Remember that a state describes how you are in body and mind at a given moment. Examples of states you may be in include confident, joyful, angry, or calm.

EXERCISE 7: USING THE CIRCLE OF EXCELLENCE TO ACCESS INNER RESOURCES

Use this exercise to get from where you are — perhaps a negative state, such as angry, to a positive state, such as centered and calm — using the Circle of Excellence pattern.

Step 1: First, look for triggers. What are the visual, auditory, or kinesthetic cues that led to the negative state? Maybe you always become upset when you hear a certain word, phrase, or sound that your spouse or partner makes.

Step 2: Next, draw an imaginary circle on the floor. Think of a time when you felt centered and calm. Allow the memory to help you experience the same feelings right now.

Step 3: As you continue experiencing the positive feelings, step into the circle. As you move into the circle, begin to recall the anchors that precede the negative state. The key is to hold onto the positive feelings while simultaneously recalling the negative triggers. If you have sufficiently amplified your positive state, it will feel more powerful than the negative triggers. The negative triggers will thus be extinguished.

Using NLP in personal life is largely about how well you can communicate with others and with yourself. You can improve communication with others primarily by always working to build rapport. Teachers, parents, supervisors, and others should be interested in building rapport because it reduces resistance and increases cooperation. Rapport also fosters feelings of connection and trust.

CASE STUDY:
THE BENEFITS OF NLP

Brian Stone
Master Practitioner NLP
Developer of Systemic
Behavioral Dynamics™
612-387-1969

My experience with NLP began in 2002 when I embarked on a personal journey of self-improvement. I began by reading several self-help books and even sought help from several therapists without much relief. While continuing to do research, I encountered something significant online — a discipline called NLP. I began studying it diligently and using it with myself and others right away. From finding out that the most famous self-help gurus had been trained in this discipline, I decided to get trained as well. I received my practitioner certification, and then I received my master practitioner certification from Tad James. Tad James is founder and CEO of the Tad James Co., an NLP training company, with more than 25 years of experience in NLP training and education.

I began practicing NLP immediately that year. I have used NLP for seven years. I am a believer that it is possible to get a lot out of working with a qualified teacher with a strong philosophy that guides them, but it is almost impossible for a newcomer to learn and discern those things.

The basic techniques and patterns I believe to be most important for those learning NLP would be the anchoring technique, collapse anchoring technique, and the fast Phobia Cure pattern. These are great processes for helping a beginner learn how to influence and shift the cognitive processes within another person. I believe it will increase the user's confidence and help him or her simultaneously place his or her faith where it needs to be: in the people and the minds they help.

I use many of the principles of NLP in my practice while working with clients, but I have since expanded beyond my understanding of NLP and am now guided by an advanced discipline I have developed called Systemic Behavioral Dynamics™. NLP had provided wonderful and comprehensive tools, but it seemed lacking in providing a way to think about their application. Systemic Behavioral Dynamics picks up where NLP leaves off.

I use both the Milton model and the meta model so often now that I do not even realize I am doing it. I find them to be tools that fit some situations and not others. They are not absolute, but nothing in NLP is.

Anchoring is critical in the NLP process because more than being a technique, it actually serves as a metaphor for what our purpose with clients is: to have them experience a completely different associative reaction with the cognitive material that used to perpetuate negative feelings and decisions.

A typical NLP session is unlike traditional therapy. Traditional therapy seems to rely on the therapist asking questions and having faith that the client will be able to "fix" him or herself by reviewing his or her awful experiences again through the telling of the story. Though I believe that therapists by and large provide a wonderful and much needed service and help many people, by the time they come to someone like me, those "traditional" methods have not worked. So, we spend a minimal amount of time talking about content and having the client rehash the details of his or her personal crises. We talk just enough for me to discover how he or she is processing the information, and then I use different tools and techniques at my disposal to help him or her gain immediate relief from the problem.

The most important benefits of NLP are that it brings an order and substance to the cognitive processes that help us to experience being happy or sad. It helps to bring a focus to the process part of our experience and, therefore, gives something that can be focused on and shifted in the moment and with immediate results verified in the client's own personal experience.

What most people look for from NLP is the same thing they look for from traditional therapists: hope that they can get relief from their problems and experience life in a better and fuller way. I believe they look for someone or something to help them make sense of their life and their experience and hope to find satisfying answers to the questions of why, what, and how of their life's questions. My own illusions about the "sacred" knowledge that therapist's hold disintegrated when I was able to have private sessions with some as clients and discover they were in fact just as much in search of satisfying answers as many of the clients they see. We all search for the same things, and with NLP and newer disciplines like Systemic Behavioral Dynamics, I think we all get a little closer.

I personally use NLP and the tools from it on a daily basis. I think the most noticeable effect it has had are in the areas of both how I communicate with others and what I expect from people in general. I now have learned to communicate and take responsibility for how the communication is received between the recipient and me, as well the myriad of tools available to enhance the delivery and reception of my messages. Second, my expectations of human behavior have shifted to allow for an understanding of why, how, and what things collectively and individually motivate behavior. In short, I understand people much better than I ever have before.

NLP can offer the most benefits to those working with people, and because I believe the field offers many insights into how to get a better experience from life, I believe that the sooner someone uses it the better. NLP is particularly useful for teachers of all types, especially those who work with children. Doctors as well are in a unique position of authority to be able to utilize influence with much more precision and with life-altering results.

NLP is just as effective in personal relationships as it is in professional relationships. It can be of use in both situations because of its perspective that teaches a person to be responsive to what is important to the other person's viewpoint, values, and beliefs.

I find the most effective ways to build and use rapport to be pacing, body language and verbal pacing, and keyword tracking to make sure you begin communicating in an immediate rhythm with the other person.

NLP is a more conscious process than hypnotherapy, but both access the unconscious so I do not think of them so much as separate things and more like two measures on a continuum. Hypnotherapy leans more on the side of the unconscious change processes, and NLP leans more toward the side of the conscious awareness in the spectrum of change modalities.

I believe all great truths are simple, and because of this, I think that when a person embarks on his or her journey of self-discovery and begins to learn NLP, he or she discovers that it seems "intuitive." I have found that NLP mimics their own personal experiences and sheds light on the same unconscious and cognitive processes that they themselves have had to go through in their own life. I do believe, like in any field, once the foundation is achieved, those brave and creative few can and will venture beyond the things written and will of course be ultimately responsible for the expansion of the field.

I have a year's worth of success stories. One is from a woman who drove several hours just to see me, based on a referral from her sister. She came with challenges of chronic pain in her wrists and hands, depression, negative beliefs about herself, and a failing home life because of her inability to be present and attentive as a mother and to connect with her husband. The pain in her wrists and hands threatened her job because she had spent extended time off work. We had only one session together to get her relief, and we did. She left without the depression, with an increased level of personal confidence, ready to take on the world again, and connect with her husband, and the pain had greatly diminished, if not disappeared completely. Though I attribute the success to her personal willingness to change and help heal herself, I was glad to not only guide her on that journey but to also have heard two years later that she still had no recurrence of her former problems.

I do not respond to criticism that NLP is not supported by science because I do not care. To be precise, it is not that I do not care about science, because I love it, but even science is not supported by science at times. And as a culture, we need to remember we all benefit from the comfort that static rules and the unchangeable standards that science seems to offer but in truth never really has. In my opinion, science is observation of and manipulation of the knowns and the exploration of the unknowns as well. That is all it is. Science is the observation and cataloging of knowns and unknowns mixed with the manipulation of those things in order to learn. If science's background is truly built around learning, then it should embrace NLP because neither NLP nor science is infallible, and both are still young and have a lot of growing to do.

I believe that NLP is still in its young phases, and I think that it represents a doorway to something even more profound and enriching. Do not stop; keep going in discovery and exploration. It was once believed that the sun revolved around the Earth, which is proof that if science can be wrong and learn from its mistakes and grow so can NLP. I do not believe the pursuit is about perfection but rather about always getting closer to some greater truth, perhaps a greater one than can be fathomed by our minds, but we are empowered in the journey itself.

Chapter 3

THE PILLARS OF NLP

The previous chapters have discussed rapport. Rapport, along with sensory acuity, behavioral flexibility, and outcome thinking, form the four pillars of NLP. These pillars form the basis for the NLP philosophy, and these pillars support all NLP concepts. Emphasis on pillars during communication is important because they reduce or eliminate miscommunication and increase mutual understanding.

Behavioral Flexibility

As the word flexibility suggests, this pillar is concerned with one's ability to adapt his or her actions as a strategy for influencing a particular response from and in response to another person. Behavioral flexibility allows you to feel comfortable with diverse groups of people and in a variety of circumstances because your behavior is motivated by a desire to influence, understand, connect, and build rapport. Behavioral flexibility is much like redirecting your course; it allows you to change course or choose different ways of relating to others if your actions do not lead you in the intended direction. For example, being flexible with behavior can be as simple as moving to stand closer to someone who seems upset. It can also look like adjusting a training format to increase interaction if participants do not seem responsive. The key with behavioral flexibility is noticing the level of responsiveness, deciding if it is high enough, and if not, adapting behavior to improve results.

Sensory Acuity

Can you tell what a person thinks and feels before he or she even says a word? You can see it in his or her eyes or maybe the way the person holds the shoulders or positions the arms. You can use your senses to assess the efficacy of communication. Paying attention to small changes in facial expression or eye movement helps you determine if what you are saying resonates with or annoys others. It is important to note here that body language is as unique as individuals themselves. Though it is true that some signals, such as crossed arms, may mean the same thing for many people, most meanings should be discovered and interpreted through active observation.

This rule is particularly important when interacting with people who may not share your cultural background. Do not make assumptions about what you see. Continue to check what you see against what you hear and feel. This is called calibration, a sort of fine-tuning process that helps you get in sync during communication. Think of this process similarly to how you might think of each instrument of an orchestra tuning to one pitch. Tuning allows the instruments to play together in harmony. In interactions, calibration or tuning allows each person to follow the pitch or cue for better communication.

Rapport

You may recall the presupposition, "The meaning of your communication is the response you get." When there is misunderstanding or resistance, the likely reason is lack of rapport. The goal in creating rapport is not wholesale agreement of everything that is being communicated but rather to show the other person you understand what he or she is trying to communicate.

You have no doubt shared a conversation that just flowed or met someone and felt you had known each other for years. If so, then you understand rapport. It is the difference between a conversation that feels awkward or uncomfortable and one that does not. When you notice the conversation is uncomfortable, use the pillars of NLP, as well as the individual's output channels, to begin building rapport.

The output channels are words, voice, and body. To get a full understanding of what is communicated, you must survey, interpret, and respond to all three output channels.

1. The words:

- Does the person use expressions that feel familiar to you?

- Which sensory words does the person use?

2. The voice:

- How loud or soft is the person's voice?

- What can you tell from the tone of voice?

- Is he or she speaking fast or slow?

3. The body:

- How are the arms and legs positioned?

- What gestures are being used?

- How has the speaker positioned his or her body in relation to yours?

- What can you learn from his or her facial expressions?

UCLA Professor Emeritus of Psychology Albert Mehrabi-an assigned weights or values to each of the three output channels. Born in 1939, Mehrabian's studies of commu-nication led to what is today known as the 7%-38%-55% rule. In short, words account for 7 percent of communica-tion, while voice and body account for 38 percent and 55 percent, respectively.

The message is not that words do not matter; they do. In-stead, the message is that words must be congruent with tone of voice and body language to build rapport. You can-not build rapport or connection when communicating in-congruently. You will recall that congruence in communi-cation is another way of saying that your words match your behavior and tone of voice. When your words do not match your body language or tone of voice, the listener will ulti-mately take his or her cues about what you are really think-ing and feeling from your voice and body, not your words. For example, if Bill offers a compliment to his co-worker in a sarcastic tone, his co-worker will most likely discount the words and take meaning from Bill's tone. Likewise, if Ann offers sympathetic words to a grieving neighbor while smil-ing or laughing, her neighbor will experience Ann's words as false because they are incongruent or do not match her body language.

You cannot hope to build rapport without some attention and response to these outputs from the first perceptual po-sition — your own. You must also maintain an awareness of your own outputs and how the listener receives and interprets them. You should respond to outputs by matching or mirroring what you see and hear. In doing this, you are not behaving like a copycat; rather, you are sending a signal or demonstrating a pattern that the listener will recognize as familiar. The practice of matching another person's predicates — words that reveal how he or she represents things in his or her consciousness, behavior, speech, and posture — is called pacing. *Chapter 2 also discussed pacing for rapport.*

Outcome Thinking

Outcome thinking encourages you to clearly define what you want so you are more likely to get it. How, you ask? Clarity cuts through confusion and directs energy with laser focus on the desired outcome. Outcome thinking helps you shift from the problem to the process of considering solutions. Attention to the problem occupies your internal resources, making them unavailable to fully focus on the solution. Think about the last time you were faced with a problem. Chances are you spent a lot of time and energy feeling angry, anxious, puzzled, or frustrated about the problem. You probably turned it over in your mind many times. Before you knew it, the problem seemed even larger, and you probably felt emotionally exhausted. Outcome thinking focuses resources on the solution, thus changing your frame of mind from stuck to possible. For example, suppose your children do not help around the house. Immediately shift your focus to what you want instead. Say to yourself, "I want the children to help with the dishes, laundry, and the dog." Then, start working on how to get to the desired outcome. For example, would using a rewards system work? Are the children getting up early enough to let the dog out? Would the children help with the laundry if you stopped doing their laundry for them? Choose a plan to work toward your outcome and fine tune it until you consistently get the outcome you want.

The pillars of NLP form the building blocks for successful communication. As you begin noticing your own responses and the responses of others, you will more easily build rapport. It is impossible to positively lead, influence, or connect with others without first building rapport. Practice using these skills until they become natural for you. Do not worry if it feels awkward at first. Remember that learning a new skill occurs in four phases: subconscious incompetence (where you do not have the skill or even an awareness of the skill deficit), conscious incompetence (an awareness of the skill deficit), conscious competence (awareness and emerging skill development), and subconscious competence (the skill is mastered and feels like second nature).

As you work toward subconscious competence by becoming a master communicator, know you are building the foundation for ongoing success in your personal and professional life.

As you continue to build communication skills, remember the pillars of NLP. This might take time and practice. It does not matter if you do not remember the names of each of the pillars in the beginning. What is most important is to notice how the listener is responding with words and body language to what you, the speaker, are saying. Use that information to adapt your words, voice, and body until you begin to feel rapport building.

A final note about the pillars of NLP: Each is much like the tools you might use in carpentry or the kitchen. They are like your hammer and nail or your knife and salt — essential for your craft.

Chapter 4

FOCUS ON THE OUTCOME FRAME

Most everyone sets goals. Sometimes the goals people set are simple and easy to achieve. For example, someone might set a goal to read one book each month. Other goals are more complex, like learning to speak another language. No matter the kind of goal, a focus on the outcome frame offers a more nuanced way of thinking about and approaching the goal. The outcome frame brings a complete picture, including the feelings involved, of completing the goal into clear focus.

Your focus on the outcome frame is much like blueprints are to a house you might build. Well-designed blueprints improve the chances for a well-built house. Blueprints also provide an opportunity to create a visual representation of the physical house. In other words, you see the house before it becomes real; you know where each room is positioned and have given some thought to design. Now, think of the house without the blueprints. Chances are the house will not be structurally sound or even possible to build without first spending time on the blueprints.

Outcome Frame Defined

In the simplest terms, an outcome is a developed goal, desire, or dream. The previous example of learning to speak another language articulates a desire or goal; it does not consider how the goal can be achieved or even if it is possible. NLP provides a model for transforming goals into outcomes. A goal becomes an outcome after five conditions have been met.

Five conditions for transforming goals into outcomes

1. **The goal must be stated in positive terms.** In other words, the goal should identify what you want or value. According to Dr. Norman Vincent Peale, author of *The Power of Positive Thinking*, positive thinking leads to confidence, success, and achievement. Peale, a Protestant preacher who died in 1993 at the age of 95, is widely acknowledged as founder of the practice and idea of positive thinking. Positive thinking is strongly supported in NLP.

Example: "I want to learn to speak another language." This goal is stated in positive terms.

The goal should not state what you do not want.

Example: "I do not want to feel like an idiot when I travel abroad without speaking the language." This goal is stated in negative terms.

There is an advantage to stating a goal in positive terms. Stating something in the negative suggests you have to "get through" something. The idea of getting through something can feel draining and use energy you could put toward the accomplishment. Stating something in the positive suggests you "can do" something. Feeling you can do something is empowering and energy producing. You can use that energy toward accomplishing your outcome.

2. **The goal must be sensory-based.** A sensory-based goal connects you to the outcome by allowing you to use your senses to describe how it feels to achieve what you want. Using your senses to experience your goal engages your subconscious mind in support of the outcome. When your subconscious mind embraces the outcome, feelings of resistance, and the resulting self-sabotage, are greatly reduced or eliminated.

Example: See yourself traveling on the train in the country you will visit. Feel the delight of enjoying the casual conversations you hear. Or, see yourself confidently asking about good places to visit for dinner. Feel how good it is to know what to say.

Chapter 2 discussed the importance of mind-body alignment. The mind and body are related and do not operate independently of one another. Sensory-based goals align bodies with their minds in support of that goal. It is impossible to achieve any goal without cooperation from both.

3. **The goal must be one you value and can control.** Your interest in achieving the goal must come from your unique personal motivation or mission. Your personal mission speaks to larger life questions, such as who you are or want to be in relation to the world; what you think your purpose is; what you intend to accomplish in support of this purpose; and what you want to be able to say about your life and the way you choose to live it. The goal should not be one you only think you should achieve based on the people, fads, or pressures around you. In other words, the goal should not be in response to what is happening around you; instead it should be an answer for the motivations within you.

Example: "I want to learn Chinese because it is a popular language right now." The goal is properly stated in positive terms, but it does not meet the conditions for an outcome because it does not identify a personal motivation for achieving the goal. The example goal as stated would only be useful if the motivation is to be and do what is popular.

Example: "I want to learn Chinese because I plan to live in China for a year to study." The goal is properly stated in positive terms, and it identifies a personal motivation, being prepared to study in China, for accomplishment.

You should also be able to rely exclusively, or almost exclusively, on your own actions to achieve your goal. In other words, achieving the goal should be within your control. If you are travelling abroad with a spouse or friend, it is reasonable to set a goal of learning another language. Learning another language is within your control. It would not be reasonable to set a goal that you and your spouse or friend learn another language because you have no control over whether he or she will achieve the goal.

Example: Actions I can take to achieve my goal of learning Chinese include: enrolling in a class, hiring a tutor, buying and studying language tapes, and using a language learning computer software program, DVD, or podcast. You can also set up a study schedule and make a calendar to make sure you do not schedule events that conflict with your lessons.

4. **The goal should have a context.** You can contextualize your goal by asking questions that clarify the circumstances of the outcome. Providing context for your goal is much like giving the goal an anchor in reality.

Example:

- **When** will you know you have accomplished your goal? I will accomplish my goal of learning another language when I can confidently converse in that language. I will accomplish my goal of learning another language **when** I can read a Chinese language newspaper or understand Chinese radio.
- **Who** and **where** questions are also helpful for contextualizing a goal. For example, **who** will be a part of celebrating, supporting, or benefiting from your goal; **who** will be present as you accomplish your goal? Do not be shy about naming the specific people who will be involved. For example, **who** will be in your study group? **Who** will provide child care while you study? How will you celebrate, and with **whom**, once the goal has been accomplished? Remember, you want to have the internal experience of the accomplishment, as vividly as possible, when you plan for a successful outcome.

- **Where** will you derive the most benefit from your achievement? Will the accomplishment be most helpful in your personal or professional life? **Where** will you work toward your achievement? On a practical level, you should know where in your home you will be able to concentrate while you study.

5. **The goal should fit your individual values, needs, and interests.** Your goals are as personal as your shoes. Your motivation, resources, approach, rewards, and obstacles are uniquely yours. Additionally, the goal should not be at odds with the values, needs, and interests of the systems — i.e. family, faith community, work environment — around you. You are part of a larger community. Your actions impact the people around you. When your actions adversely impact the systems you are a part of, the resulting feelings may cause you to abandon your goals.

   Example: Enrolling in a language class using money you need for your car payment or time you must dedicate for child care may be at odds with your personal or family values, needs, and interests. You can manage these obstacles by selling your car if you can find reliable, alternative transportation, hiring child care to free up time to attend class, or choosing an online or DVD study program rather than an in-person class.

Evaluating needs, values, and interests early can eliminate obstacles and pitfalls later. This information can help you develop a workable plan you are less likely to abandon. For example, what resources do you already have in place? What resources do you need? Here, you will want to consider material resources — such as things like a DVD player — and internal resources — such as skills, knowledge, and confidence.

Recall the presupposition, "People have all the resources they need." Name all of the resources you can think of that you will need to meet your outcome. Begin with internal resources. You will be able to access the resources you need even if you do not feel immediately connected to them.

Internal resources for achieving outcomes

Learning another language might require confidence. Confidence is an example of an internal resource. Try to think of another time you needed confidence to accomplish something that felt very big. Even if you do not feel very confident when you begin Chinese lessons, you can achieve the useful state of confidence by practicing the Swish pattern. *See Chapter 2 for more on this pattern.* You might also use an anchor to bring about a state of confidence each time you begin a lesson. We have discussed anchors often. Triggering an anchor can help you move from a non-useful state, such as lacking confidence, to a useful one, such as feeling confident in your ability to learn Chinese.

Discipline or staying on task can also be an internal resource. If you find it difficult to study when your favorite program is on television, it will be important to decide whether you are appropriately motivated to achieve your outcome. If you have checked your motivation and found that it answers a question or need that comes from within, you might simply need a quick run through of the Godiva Chocolate pattern exercise to stay on track. *See Chapter 2, Exercise 5 for more information on this pattern.*

Material or external resources for achieving outcomes

You will also need to consider what material resources are available to you in support of your goal. For example, whether you have, or can get, a DVD player will impact the kind of study-at-home language program you choose. If you choose a study group or class, you will need to consider how you will get to those meetings. For example, do you have the money for gas or public transit? Can you carpool to the class, or is it feasible to start a study group at work or school?

Your goals are the seeds of your outcomes. They are ideas that must be developed and nurtured to be transformed into actual achievements. Another way of thinking about the important difference between goals and outcomes is to think about the difference between saying you want to start a business and developing a business plan for your entrepreneurial venture. The first example is simply a stated desire; there is no energy, thought, or movement toward completion of the goal associated with the statement. The second example provides an opportunity to consider and develop the desire, determine if it is possible, determine what it would take to be successful, and what resources would be required to start a business.

Each of the five conditions is important for achieving a goal by first developing that goal into an outcome. In terms of prioritizing the conditions, the first condition — "State the goal in positive terms" — is perhaps the most important. Nothing else you do toward achieving the outcome will matter if you do not believe the outcome is possible for you.

Turn your goals into accomplishments by exploring them with the five conditions in mind. As you begin, consider using a journal to write down your plans and chart your progress. You might also consider talking with friends or family members to be sure you have not overlooked an obstacle or resource. Be clear about your motivations; it can help to write them down. Finally, remember to circle dates on a calendar you see regularly and include dates by each of the steps that lead you to your goal. Your success will be virtually guaranteed.

CASE STUDY: LIFE TRANSFORMATIONS WITH NLP

Jaime Rojas
Certified Life Coach though the
society of NLP as a master coach
www.positivelystrong.com

I was introduced to NLP by Tony Robbins about six years ago. I have been certified for five years and deal with an average of five clients each day. My experience has been fantastic in the sense that the changes are huge and often happen in a matter of minutes. But, I have noticed some aspects of peeling the onion, if you will, that sometimes require additional work. For example, the minute my clients have gotten down to the root of their issue, their uncertainty sometimes becomes higher because they realize they are in the wrong career or have chosen the wrong spouse. At this point, they have made agreements with themselves and others they do not believe they can break. Breaking those agreements can be the toughest thing to do. I had a client who I will call Maria. She came to me because she felt she needed a motivation anchor. Maria had wanted to break the record of paddling a surfboard from Cuba to the coast of Florida, a 90-mile trip in shark-infested waters. That is some accomplishment, right?

I began by talking with her to understand her world and how it was represented for her. Maria was born into a very religious family. She had been feeling very insignificant lately because she had just found the courage to tell her mother she was gay. Her mother rejected her and kicked her out of her home. Accomplishing this feat was significant, even if it would cost her life, because she had convinced herself and other people around her that she was doing it for charity purposes. In reality, she created this goal to meet her need for significance, especially in her mother's eyes.

I have had the privilege of working with children as young as 6 years old, a 21 year old who had felt suicidal, and even a 60 year old. NLP is effective across age groups. The techniques make it so easy to establish rapport. You can establish rapport in literally five minutes. A typical session involves stepping into my client's world to connect with them every time. Of course, listening is key to building rapport and to keep on doing it to deal with the particular issue of the day.

The pattern I have found so far is it takes anywhere from one to 12 sessions to make radical changes in behavior. I especially enjoy hearing from clients months later to thank me and let me know how much better they feel. This work is very fulfilling. Usually people think, "Just help me deal with this issue," when in reality they do not know what the real issue is.

I feel the real benefit of NLP is the ability to create the game of life in a winnable way. NLP allows my clients to get rid of all of those fears they learned and to reconnect with that spiritual aspect of themselves. That is why I use these strategies every day in my own life with family members and friends. I also use NLP when delivering speeches to connect with my audience because it gives you the edge to influence anyone from business associates to your date or spouse.

My life has been completely transformed thanks to NLP — especially when I was trying to kill myself years ago. Learning to understand how my brain processed information was the biggest shift in my life. I am grateful to Grinder and Bandler.

The simplest way to build rapport is to do as Steven Covey advises: Listen with the intention to understand and not with the intention to reply because right there you are eliciting needs, modalities, models of the world, and metaprograms. These ideas are related to hypnotherapy, especially as it relates to Erickson's work. We are communicating to the unconscious all the time. The minute you understand this concept, it becomes second nature, much like tying your shoes — you do not think about it; it just happens.

For me, anchoring is the most effective technique out there. The meta model and the Milton model create linkages by using words. Both are very effective, especially when coupled with anchoring concepts with my clients and friends.

Back to Maria the athlete — we worked together to change the meaning or the representation that life was only about achievement to the idea that life was a playground. I believe everyone can use these skills to influence themselves and then other people. That is why I recommend people investigate NLP to learn how it can help them create the changes they really want.

You do not need certification to enjoy the benefits of NLP. But, when it comes to dealing with fears and phobias, the right coaching can make the difference. For those critics who are skeptical or say NLP does not work, I say they are wrong. At the end of the day, there is plenty of evidence to prove NLP does work. The success I have witnessed in my clients is indisputable.

NLP Application: Fun Uses for NLP

"WILL IT SELL? FILTERS FOR NONFICTION SUBMISSIONS"

Used with permission from Leigh Steere

Confession: I am not a fellow publisher or an author. Instead, I am a bookworm with a background in neuro-linguistics, which explores the relationship between language and attention.

At any given moment, my nightstand is cluttered with a wide array of books. Right now? *Animorphs #20, Peacemaker Student Edition. Outliers*, a "Star Wars" early reader on podracing. *Three Cups of Tea*, a book on menopause, and one on management. Eclectic, eh? (I have three kids.)

I am fairly patient, and I am willing to plow through less-than-engaging tomes to extract pearls of wisdom from subject-matter experts. But, my patience has a limit. If I start drifting off in the middle of a page — and if that happens several times — I have a rule of thumb.

I stop reading and donate the book to the library fundraising shelf. Some other poor soul might have the same dry reading experience but at least the library will be a dollar richer.

We live in a time-strapped culture where we carefully weigh how to use our precious moments of free time. "Entertainment value" has become a major selection criterion for how we spend our money and time off — and for how we select nonfiction books.

Out of curiosity, and because of my neuro-linguistics training, I recently examined some yawner books to determine why they were not engaging. In the process, I found two filters that publishers can use in selecting and editing nonfiction manuscripts.

TEST FOR SPINOUT

Definition: "Spinout" occurs when a reader mentally leaves the text to process information and then does not return to finish reading the text.

Technical explanation: Neuro-linguistic practitioners teach a technique for listening and coaching that involves using non-sensory specific language to ask questions or invite people to consider new information. For example, a listener might ask:

- What do you think should happen next?

- What do you recommend?

- What thoughts come to mind when you consider this information?

These sample questions do not contain strongly visual, auditory, or kinesthetic language. They are sensory generic and invite the responder to access all representation systems in formulating an answer. As a result:

- The listener normally gets a richer response.

- The responder sometimes gets lost in rich thought.

In one-on-one settings, if responders get lost in thought, listeners can pull them back to the conversation with a follow-up question, such as, "You seem to be processing something. Can you share what's on your mind?"

But, what happens if a sensory-generic question or statement in a book prompts the reader to get lost in rich thought? Sometimes, the reader does not return to the text.

Example: "Both overuse their natural style and become less effective."

Diagnosis: This sentence is concise, clear, and technically perfect. But, can you make a picture of what this means in your mind? Or can you imagine how it sounds or feels? No. It is sensory generic and poses a risk for spinout.

When readers spin out, those who do not absolutely need the information in a book may set the book aside. These readers might conclude — consciously or unconsciously — that the book is taking too long to read, and they might opt for another book or activity. They might decide the book is "dry" and not recommend it to others.

Rx: If you find yourself spinning out while reading a nonfiction manuscript, look carefully at the language. If it is sensory generic, you can determine how much effort will be required to infuse visual, auditory, and kinesthetic language. By shifting the balance between types of illustrations and language, you may increase the book's chances of success.

By the way, you probably spun out a little bit while reading this section. How did it feel?

Chapter 5

UNDERSTANDING COMMUNICATION

P oor communication is equally a problem in professional and personal settings. Recall the presuppositions, "You cannot not communicate" and "The
meaning of communication is the response you get."
Communication encompasses so much more than the
words you speak. Even when you choose silence, the
people around you are interpreting what they do not
hear and what they see. What is important to remember
about communication is you are always communicating
or transmitting messages. If you want to communicate
effectively, you will tailor your messages based on the responses they elicit.

Communication happens when you interact with or come into contact with others. There is another way of communicating that many do not often think about. In addition to communicating with others, you communicate with yourself. There is an almost constant dialogue taking place between mind and body. That dialogue guides your thoughts, feelings, decisions, and actions.

How Do We Communicate?

One of the ways you communicate is through representational systems, also called sense modalities. Your representational, or rep system, helps you recognize the information that comes in through your senses. You may gain this information with your sense of smell or your sight. You can also take information in by tasting, hearing, or feeling. You use this information in many ways. For example, you can use information you take in through your senses to understand what happens around you and to make decisions about actions you might take.

It is important to understand representational systems because they are useful in improving your communication with others and with yourself. You already know that representational systems help you recognize information. For example, hearing screams might lead you to conclude someone nearby is in danger or feeling distress. Representational systems are also involved in your ability to store and recall information. Think of a vivid experience. Chances are that you recalled the experience through the senses that originally helped you define that experience. If your memory is a county fair, for example, you might remember what a beautiful day it was; you might remember the feeling of the warm sun, see the vibrant blue sky or fluffy white clouds, hear children laughing, or smell popcorn. Your representational system helps you take in, interpret, store, and recall all of the information or messages around you.

Representational systems help you recall experiences. The power of NLP is in its encouragement to use representational systems to also create experiences. The same sense modes discussed previously — sight, sound, taste, smell, and feeling — can be employed to create an experience in your mind that you would like to have in your life. The idea here is to use your representational system to create an experience that feels so real it becomes almost like a memory or something that has already happened. As the experience becomes more real, any resistance to achieving it lessens and motivation to achieve it grows. You can use your representational system to create the experiences you value. The way you think about an experience will determine how you respond to the experience. Using all or most of your senses produces a very strong response and leads to higher motivation. Conversely, using one or few senses will produce a weaker response and is not likely to facilitate high motivation to achieve the experience.

The dominant rep system varies with different individuals *(See Chapter 3)*. To determine the rep system or sense mode being used, watch for predicates and/or eye accessing cues.

Predicates

NLP uses predicates to describe the clues that reveal the representational system being used. Predicates can be verbal or nonverbal. Verbal predicates include terms like "I hear," "I feel," or "I see." Nonverbal predicates include gestures or body language. These nonverbal clues also offer valuable information that reveals what is thought or felt. Watch and listen for predicates to understand the representational system being used.

The next time you are engaged in conversation, watch and listen to notice the primary representational system (PRS) being used. For example, someone with a visual PRS might talk about a vacation using words that describe what he or she saw, such as the lush green trees; another person with an auditory PRS might remember the sound of the ocean or the crickets at night. Most people use all of the representational systems with one system being more dominant than the others. Another way to look for the PRS being used is to notice nonverbal predicates. Nonverbal predicates are observable cues to the PRS being used. In the vacation example, the speaker describing his or her vacation with visual words might first look up while accessing the words. The person with the auditory primary representational system might begin by looking to the side. *For a more detailed discussion, see Exercise 3 in Chapter 2.*

How can predicates improve communication?

Predicates tell you something about the dominant sense being used to understand and interpret information. One of the primary goals of successful communication is building rapport. Identifying the representational system being used by listening for and matching the predicate is an easy way to build rapport. Matching predicates is simply using words that demonstrate identification with the rep system being used. For example, you can match predicates with someone who demonstrates an auditory sense mode by leaning your ear in close while he or she speaks, and by using words that conjure up sound images. Use words that create an image when you want to match predicates with a verbal person. If appropriate, you can also use charts, graphs, and pictures. Matching predicates suggests to the other person that you understand his or her feelings and motivations, thus creating feelings of trust and rapport.

Eye-accessing cues

The next time you talk with someone watch his or her eyes. Almost everyone unconsciously moves his or her eyes while talking and listening. This eye movement is an external sign that information is being considered or processed internally. Watching how the eyes move is a clue to how the information is being processed. NLP calls these techniques eye-accessing cues. The movement and direction of the eyes tells whether someone is hearing or seeing images or even experiencing feelings internally. *See Exercise 3 in Chapter 2 for more information about interpreting eye-accessing cues.*

EXERCISE 8: USING NLP TO IMPROVE CONVERSATIONAL OUTCOMES

All of us have had the experience of talking with someone who was difficult or with whom it seemed we would never find any common ground. Use the following steps to improve conversational outcomes in even the most challenging environments.

Step 1: Determine the outcome. Begin by spending a few moments to clarify what you hope to achieve with the conversation. In other words, what do you want the outcome to be? Do you want agreement or cooperation? Are you hoping the other person will see your point of view, agree to perform a task, sign a contract, or make a gift to your organization? Be clear about your outcome, which is much like a destination. You must know where you want to go so you will know when you have accomplished what you set out to do at the start of the conversation.

Step 2: Decide on plan B. Consider the need for a plan B. For this example, we will assume you are negotiating with a company to win a signed sales contract. Plan B will be the difference between the best-case scenario and the good-enough scenario. An example of these scenarios might be the following:

Best case: You get a signed sales contract for five years of service.

Good enough: You get a signed contract for one year of service.

It can also be useful to consider a plan C. Do you abandon the whole project if you cannot get to your desired conversational outcome? Absolutely not; this is a perfect opportunity to reframe. So, you do not get agreement, but maybe you do get a better understanding that will pave the way for a contract in the future.

Step 3: Determine which emotional state you need to be successful. Choose your most resourceful emotional state. How will you need to feel and what will you need to think as you begin and continue the conversation? If you are talking with a particularly difficult person, it will probably be important to feel calm and patient. If you are talking with an angry or aggressive person, you might want to appear confident. And if you are talking with someone that has doubts about what you are saying, you might want to come across as knowledgeable and reassuring. Remember that you can easily access the desired state by firing an anchor to trigger that state. Take a few moments to visualize yourself having the conversation in your desired state. See the body language you will use, your words, as well as your tone of voice.

Step 4: Look for clues to build rapport. Remember to continue building rapport as you converse. Respond to the PRS (preferred representational system) of the person you are talking with. You should also understand something about how she or he is motivated — for example, toward or away from. Someone with a "toward" motivation takes action to gain something or with a payoff in mind; for example, this kind of person wants to get to work early because he or she likes to enjoy a relaxing cup of coffee before beginning the work day. An individual with an "away from" motivation takes action to avoid something. This person gets to work early because he or she does not want to be fired.

Step 5: Consider the second perceptual position. Adopt the other person's point of view or perceptual position. What is he or she thinking and feeling about what is being communicated?

Step 6: Acknowledge areas of agreement. Look for and point to any areas of general agreement to build on. For example, you might both agree it is important for nonprofits to use donor-tracking software. This can be a starting place from which to build agreement on the price and brand of donor-tracking software.

Step 7: Clarify and wrap up the discussion. Review what you have discussed and decided, and plan the next steps. These may include an outline of what you can expect over the next several weeks or months. For example, if any tasks were decided upon, who will do what and by when?

Recall the presupposition, "You cannot not communicate." Communication is at the heart of every relationship, even the most casual or fleeting ones, such as between you and the cashier at your local grocery store. Both of you will take something away from that exchange based on what you see and hear. The value of understanding communication is at least twofold. First, you can decide the kind of messages you want to communicate, and second, you can practice the skills you need to communicate intended messages across a variety of settings. Communicating unintended messages results in conflict and misunderstanding. When you understand communication, you can tailor your words and delivery to create rapport or a positive interaction with virtually anyone. This kind of skilled communication is the basis for charisma, meaningful connection, and ultimately, rapport.

CASE STUDY:
THE BENEFITS OF NLP

Leigh Steere
Incisive B2B and Managing
People Better, LLC
Owner of Incisive; Co-owner of
Managing People Better, LLC
www.managingpeoplebetter.com

I completed practitioner training — 27 days — and master practitioner training — 20 days — through the NLP Institute of Chicago in 1994, an affiliate of NLP Comprehensive in Colorado. I also completed trainer training at NLP Comprehensive. Shortly after, I co-purchased the company from founders Steve and Connirae Andreas and served as general manager there for 13 months. I co-developed and co-taught a class at NLP Comprehensive entitled, "Marketing and Selling Your Services" (NLP-based curriculum). I have practiced NLP since January 1994.

Professionally, I have used NLP in:

- Coaching employees on job performance issues.

- Providing career counseling.

- Interviewing prospective new hires.

- Solving complex conflicts.

- Branding projects to influence employee and consumer behavior.

- Analyzing messages — helping employers understand what messages employees actually received versus what messages the employers intended.

- Designing curriculum for hard- and soft-skills training.

I use NLP to help inspire attitude and behavior shifts — and to help others understand the dynamics of what happens when they do not get the behaviors or attitudes they want. I also use NLP to help people understand each other's communication style and preferences.

NLP provides comprehensive framework for understanding human communication and behavior. If I am not getting the result I want, I have a tool kit for understanding why and for formulating alternative communication approaches.

I think most people really do not know what to expect. They often sign up for an NLP class based on the recommendation of an enthusiastic friend, who is evangelizing the merits of NLP. They know their friend is excited, and they trust their friend's opinions. They become curious enough to spend the time and money to find out more. I believe many people look at NLP as an adventure into the unknown. They sign up as a leap of faith.

I use NLP every day. It is such an integrated part of how I think that I no longer consciously say, "What can I use from NLP for this situation?" In my opinion, it is an essential tool kit for self-examination and for effective communication, negotiation, and conflict resolution at home and at work. NLP is equally effective in both personal and professional settings.

Rapport happens on many levels. It starts when we mirror body language and listen and watch to understand whether a person leads with the visual, auditory, or kinesthetic representation systems — or occasionally, gustatory or olfactory. As we start communicating with a person through his or her leading representation system, rapport deepens. If we listen for metaprograms, such as "toward" or "away from" thinking, we can further deepen rapport by acknowledging through our own communication that we understand where they come from.

To use non-NLP parlance, rapport is about stepping into someone else's shoes and seeing, hearing, or feeling the world from his or her perspective. Most people tend to look through their own "lens" or "filters." NLP helps you develop the flexibility to experience the world through someone else's glasses. When we have the capacity, the ability to do this, we can see the root of a conflict. We can understand how to communicate in a way the audience will actually "hear" — in a way that helps our message come across as intended.

I use both the meta model and the Milton model. I do not consciously think about a distinction between the models.

I think it helps to understand if there is a current anchor holding a limiting belief or behavior in place. I do not consciously think about anchoring in my work, but I suppose I help to create new anchors through many of the communication projects I work on. If you are trying to help a person shift from behavior/attitude A to behavior/attitude B, then the process is much like a boat. You need to lift the anchor and reel it in before you can move to the next destination. Once you get to the new destination, you drop anchor to hold your position. If a boat does not lift its anchor, the anchor drags along the bottom, gets caught on things, and impedes progress and speed. The concept of anchoring is critical to NLP. Many therapists, corporate coaches, and corporate communicators inadvertently try to create change while an anchor is dragging the bottom of the waterway.

I use NLP to create new "frameworks" for helping people get their arms around complex problems. Any adult, and possibly teenagers as well, can benefit from NLP. I do not believe it is possible to learn NLP thoroughly from a book or from audio training. It is vital to engage all sensory systems in learning NLP. In a well-run training, the instructors use all modalities to teach and demonstrate nuances. They explain the concepts, provide visual demonstrations, have you practice, and provide detailed visual, auditory, and kinesthetic feedback to help you fine tune your approach. There are some concepts that a person could learn from a book and apply without further training, but a person can apply the concepts even better with in-person, highly interactive instruction.

As an example, in my practitioner training, I was paired for an exercise with a woman who had really struggled with interpersonal relationships. She was very isolated and could not figure out what to do differently. She had enrolled in the NLP class, hoping for communication skills that would help her in relationship building.

As part of the exercise, I needed to determine her leading representation system. I looked, listened, and felt for visual, auditory, and kinesthetic feedback because that is what we focused on in class. Part way through the exercise, it dawned on me: She was leading with the olfactory system, exceedingly rare for someone born and raised in the United States. Her sweetest memories were stored in her sense of smell. There is no way a book could impart the impact I experienced in this exercise. I was awash in a sense of grief for this person, as it became painfully clear why she had trouble maintaining rapport with people. I recommend NLP Comprehensive in Colorado, particularly its summer immersion trainings. People from all continents attend these intensive sessions so you get the cross-cultural experience in addition to the NLP learning.

In reply to the "not supported by science" assertions, I ask, "What do you mean by that?" Usually, I find people who say this are basing their statement on something they have heard from others. They have not really researched the question themselves.

Chapter 6

METAPROGRAMS

The word metaprogram sounds complicated and mysterious, but it is actually very easy to understand. In the simplest terms, a metaprogram is like an internal instruction manual you use to create thoughts and take actions. The word metaprogram comes from the influence of cybernetics, or the study of human control functions, on the field of NLP.

Everyone uses rules or metaprograms that tell them what to do with and how to respond to the information they take in. Metaprograms form the foundation for all mental processes. Metaprograms offer an explanation for why two people, both using a visual representational system, might arrive at different conclusions from the same information. Although both people create an internal visual representation of the information, they will come to different conclusions because they use different metaprograms or rules for how that information is assigned meaning. Consider the following example: Susan and Lucy attend a knitting class where the instructor describes and demonstrates several kinds of stitches. Susan takes in each description and demonstration, she feels excited about all the possible stitches, and she chooses one she can begin working on. Lucy has a different experience. In fact, Lucy feels so overwhelmed by all the possible stitches that she cannot make a choice at all. In this example, both Susan and Lucy "see" what is possible, but each has different rules or metaprograms for how to think about and respond to so many choices.

Metaprograms are to people what software programs are to computers. The programs use a set of rules to analyze data and drive actions. Recall the discussion about "away from versus toward" motivation direction? The "toward or away from" motivation direction is a strategy one chooses based on the information as processed in the metaprogram.

Mental Processes

Your subconscious mind always takes in and sends out information. Your metaprogram determines how that information is used. The subconscious mind stores everything you are not consciously aware of. Some kinds of information, such as background noise, moves easily from your subconscious to your conscious mind; other information does not surface in your conscious awareness. Sometimes you only know this information is there because of how it shows up in your behavior or decisions. For example, you may not be aware of a past decision you made based on something you saw or heard, such as "Talking about bad things makes them happen," but you are aware that you feel very uncomfortable when talking about bad things.

Filters that Determine How the World is Viewed

You always take in information. You take in so much information that you cannot store it all in your conscious mind. Much of the information you take in is filtered — you keep some and discard some or compact or generalize it using it as a short hand of sorts. You also distort some of the information you take in. What you do with this information will depend on language, beliefs, and decisions. For example, if someone pays you a compliment you do not agree with, such as, "You are pretty," you may choose to discard that information because you do not believe it.

Working with limiting beliefs

Sometimes your own thoughts and beliefs stand between your present state and your desired state. For example, you may want to complete a marathon, but you do not think you can really do it. One of the easiest ways to work with limiting beliefs is to look for evidence to the contrary. For example, when faced with a task you are sure you could never tackle, remember another time you tackled a seemingly impossible task. Ask someone to help you list objective facts because, in some cases, your beliefs may cause you to deny the evidence. For example, this person might point out that your recent 10K finishing time coupled with your regular training schedule points to marathon success. The witness can greatly help you.

In his book *Beliefs: Pathways to Health & Well-Being*, Dilts has distilled the process of change into one simple formula that essentially describes every NLP strategy. Take the present state — the state where you currently experience the problem — and add resources to arrive at your desired state. As mentioned previously, it is important to check within yourself for resistance or what Dilts called interference. This would be some internal objection, normally one of three types.

Common Factors in Resistance to Change

Creating change is about more than making a decision and marshaling willpower. The process of change is complex and involves the relationship between mind, body, and the systems — such as family and faith community — around you. When you meet resistance on your way to change, take time to identify the resistance so you can plan a way around it. The following are some common factors in resistance to change:

- **Reward:** A reward for resisting the change is the most common. For example, Dennis wants to quit smoking, but the smoking patio is one of the bright spots in his day at work. Although he understands the benefits of going smoke-free, he would also miss the camaraderie of the smoker's patio.

- **Lack of knowledge:** Another type of interference involves lack of knowledge. You might want to make a change, but you do not know how to do this or what to do. For example, you might have some really great ideas for a new dress, but before you can make it, you will have to learn how to sew.

- **Insufficient time:** Finally, you might become discouraged before you actually make the change because you have not given yourself the chance or enough time to make the change. Say you want to learn to play the guitar. You take lessons for a month and become discouraged that you are not yet comfortable with chords. This is not a realistic expectation to have after just a few days.

How to Use Metaprograms in NLP

Everyone has his or her own style of motivation. Understanding metaprograms helps you motivate others, as well as find your own motivation. Identifying metaprograms can also help you build rapport with others.

Common metaprograms

There are seven common programs most people employ to some degree. An explanation of each of these follows. NLP researchers have determined that people often use the same metaprogram under a variety of circumstances.

Toward versus away from

This book has discussed this metaprogram previously. Toward versus away from describes a common motivation strategy or metaprogram. As you will recall, individuals motivated in a "toward" direction take action in anticipation of a reward. Individuals motivated in an "away from" direction take action to avoid a negative consequence. Both directions have benefits and drawbacks. Although most people using this metaprogram use both directions, they will be more motivated in one direction than the other.

Proactive versus reactive

Proactive people are more likely to jump in first and consider later; these kinds of people are initiators. Reactive people are responders; they consider what is happening before jumping in. Again, both programs have advantages. In the classroom, proactive students are likely the ones that sign up to plan and organize the first annual fall harvest carnival. Reactive students would likely respond to requests for carnival volunteers. Understanding individual motivation style helps you tailor your approach to fit the metaprogram. In this instance, if you understood that Jim is reactive, you would not ask him to plan the first carnival.

Sameness versus difference

In this category, people are motivated by creating change or difference or maintaining things as they are. People with a sameness metaprogram value constancy. They like to create situations that feel familiar. Sameness should not imply that these people do not like change at all; they are likely to accept gradual changes. People motivated by difference are driven to create change. If you are making a hiring decision and plan to make several organizational changes in the next 24 months, understanding if potential hires are motivated by sameness or difference would be important.

Internal versus external

People with an internal motivation filter ideas, values, and standards through their own individual standards. As you might expect, people with external motivation derive their feedback from external sources. Parents of children with a metaprogram that values external motivation should offer a lot of praise and positive feedback to reinforce desired behaviors.

Options versus procedures

The difference here is between actively seeking options and acting by the book. The short definition of this program might sound like the difference between possibility and process. The options person is excited and motivated by all the possible ways to look at and approach a given situation. Conversely, the procedures person uses processes or rules to decide how to approach a given situation. Government workers are often stereotyped as procedure oriented. Conversely, teenagers and young adults are often thought of as options oriented; they often buck procedures and look for ways to blaze a new path.

Global versus detail

Like the word suggests, people who operate from global metaprograms prefer the big picture. These kinds of people look for the overall view and work from there, believing the details can be filled in once the general overview has been established. The opposite kind of metaprogram, detail, is motivated by smaller bits of information. Here, it is the specifics of the situation that matter and a belief that the big picture will take care of itself after the details have been addressed. If you are talking with a global person about money management, the emphasis might be on how much money he or she can save for retirement. A detailed person might be more interested in how the interest is compounded using a particular investment vehicle.

Introvert versus extrovert

You have most likely heard these words before to describe personality types. The terms have a slightly different connotation with NLP where the focus is not on the difference between having a shy or outgoing personality. Instead, the focus is on how your metaprogram leads you to restore your emotional energy. People who operate from an introvert metaprogram feel restored by alone time. These kinds of people recover from stress and other difficult emotions by spending restorative, quiet time with themselves. Extroverts find their energy in the company of others. In fact, unlike introverts, extroverts often find large groups of people energizing rather than draining.

Identifying Metaprograms

Metaprograms govern much about how you approach any task. You can identify your metaprogram simply by noticing patterns in your own behavior and thoughts. For example, if you exercise regularly because you love the energetic way it helps you feel, you are using a toward motivation. If on the other hand, you exercise regularly because you do not want to gain weight, you are operating from an away from motivation. Look at each of the previously mentioned metaprograms to understand your motivation style.

You can also listen to others to understand how they are motivated. Casual questions often reveal a great deal when you understand metaprograms. For example, simply asking someone why he or she chose their career field or what he or she like about the job can reveal a lot of information. Someone who says she went into her chosen field because she really enjoys the dynamic environment and appreciates that she never knows what to expect from one day to the next might be operating on the difference spectrum of the same versus difference metaprogram.

Although it was previously believed that metaprograms were fixed and could not be changed, it is now known based on research by Robert Dilts, a leading thinker in NLP, that this is not the case. Although there are advantages and disadvantages to each kind of metaprogram, individuals wishing to change metaprograms that feel limiting can do so. A simple strategy for doing this follows.

EXERCISE 9: CHANGING METAPROGRAMS

Metaprograms guide decisions about which perceptions will be highlighted for attention and subsequently action. If the metaprogram you use leads you to a focus that is not useful in a particular situation, you can change it.

Step 1: Target the metaprogram you want to change. In what context do you use this program? Why do you think it does not work for you? Here is an example: Carla is a big-picture or global thinker. She is not concerned with details, which bore her. Although this metaprogram works well when participating in brainstorming sessions and board meetings, it does not work when Carla needs to help employees understand what she expects from them day to day.

Step 2: Identify the more helpful metaprogram. Carla needs to fill in the big picture or give details to her employees.

Step 3: Understand why the new metaprogram is needed. Carla's motivation for making the change to a detail from a global metaprogram may be based on her desire to improve employee performance and productivity.

Step 4: Practice the new metaprogram. As you shift programs in your mind, move your physical position. For example, stand in another part of the room, or sit in a different chair. Carla should visualize the experience of providing details. How does the new metaprogram look and feel? Associate with this feeling as if it is happening in the moment. How does this new metaprogram fit with or change your identity? *See Dilts' logical levels in Chapter 2.*

Step 5: Check within for resistance or interference with your conscious goal of changing your metaprogram. Is there any part of you that receives some benefit or reward from using the old metaprogram? Is there a way to get the benefit and change the metaprogram? For example, Carla's ability to think globally fits with her self-identity as a visionary. She likes her ability to capture a room with her ideas and finds the details boring. One way Carla can reduce resistance to this change is by finding value in developing ideas and sharing the information required to realize the global picture. Carla may find that reframing is a good strategy here.

Step 6: Check once more for resistance. Did reframing remove interference with the desired change?

Step 7: Adopt the change. *Recall the four learning levels from Chapter 1.* They are:

- **Subconscious incompetence:** You do not have the skill or even an awareness that you need the skill.

- **Conscious incompetence:** You know that you do not yet have the skill, but you recognize you need the skill .

- **Conscious competence:** Your skill emerges but not yet automatic.

- **Subconscious competence:** The skill has become such a natural part of your behavior that you can do it without thinking about it.

With time, you will become subconsciously competent with the new skill.

Metaprograms are based on the internal representation of information. These programs determine your approach or strategy when making a decision or choosing an action. Understanding how you are motivated can improve outcomes and ultimately the ability to create success in your life.

CASE STUDY: HELPING CLIENTS CHANGE BEHAVIORS AND DEVELOP NEW SKILLS WITH NLP

Lee McKinney
Self-Empowerment Hypnosis
Owner, master clinical hypnotist,
advanced NLP practitioner
seh@selfempowermenthypnosis.com
www.selfempowermenthypnosis.com

I use and have used NLP to help others make change for many years and have developed my own method of inclusion along with hypnosis, decision science, and organizational behavior. My training includes membership in multiple organizations, hours of reading, seminars (including a few presented by Richard Bandler), and hands-on practice.

I have practiced NLP for about five years, slowly incorporating it into my hypnotherapy sessions. My work with clients never excludes any issue, even ones I have never encountered previously. I truly believe that if the issue is mind related, NLP can have a positive effect to lessen the impact of the issue and actually change the issue completely, thus improving the client's quality of life. I have worked with clients from ages 5 to 82. But the majority fall in the 21 to 55 age range.

Personally, I do not have a typical session. The NLP factor I use in most sessions include metaquestions to help uncover information about the client and the best way to address his or her issue for greater success. With that said, I do not decide on a well-formed outcome until I truly understand what is best for my client. I have seen practitioners follow training procedures so closely they almost become robotic in their actions. I focus on customizing the experience so my client has the best possible results.

I truly believe NLP helps make physiological change to the neuroreceptors of the brain and can help set the groundwork for fast, true change and empowerment for anyone seeking self-improvement in any area.

i have found that most people know nothing about NLP or hypnosis. The people who believe they know something about NLP seem to seek an advantage in their related field of employment to improve sales turns or to influence others around them.

I incorporate NLP techniques with self-hypnosis to control pain, as well as maintain control of my emotions and not allow others to influence my feelings or actions. I have found no true measurable difference in these areas. Your life is your life, personal and professional, and you should not try to create different selves in either setting. But, you can become the master of your life as a whole. NLP can help people feel happier, more confident, and well balanced, as well as help them master their mental state in order to best address any situation.

The areas of change or mastery are endless. They include confidence, positive attitude, self-esteem, release from past issues, development of a new outcome from negative behaviors, greater rapport (influence) with others, self-control, improved relationship building, memory improvement, and more.

I personally incorporate many tools to build rapport — matching, mirroring, sensory acuity, asking metaquestions, leading the conversation without dominating it, subtly agreeing with a client, and above all else, truly listening and being pleasant and easygoing with a client. I increase or decrease any of these areas according to the client. I do not believe rapport can be obtained by exclusively using any one method with all clients. You must be flexible and never set any method in stone.

I started learning and practicing hypnotherapy many years before NLP, and I see many similarities in both. NLP has a base of development from hypnosis. Though I have seen and met many NLP trainers/practitioners who have not trained in hypnosis formally and do not believe they have anything in common, I tend to agree with Richard Bandler in that both induce "trance" states, but hypnosis uses a formal induction. One way to show they have shared states is covert or conversational hypnosis, which is purely linguistic. Remember, hypnosis is 90 percent linguistically induced but can include physical assistance to reach that state. A good hypnotherapist pays close attention to how the suggestion is given in order to greatly enhance the acceptance rate of the client at a subconscious and/or conscience level — depending on your belief of how hypnosis works. I believe the induction and the fact that many people believe that hypnosis affects only the subconscious mind are the main components that influence the pure NLP practitioner.

Speaking from my own experience, NLP is greatly intuitive. I believe one should learn all developed techniques or patterns and then incorporate them along with personal abilities/strengths, as long as the result is positive. But, this only comes with time and experience. A new practitioner should gain a mastered understanding before deviating and must take great care when proceeding with a client. You always must be able and ready to make changes to your method to meet the client's need.

If I had to choose the most important technique or pattern available from NLP, it is gaining rapport. The majority of time in my sessions it is the Milton model. I purposely take my client into a trance state before any change work is offered. I have a natural flow into the Milton model because of my hypnosis training. But, with that said, I normally utilize anchoring, reframing, Swish pattern, association/dissociation, mapping, and perceptual positions before traditional post-hypnotic suggestion. I find that the mix of the two has outstanding results. I do use the meta model to seek information from the client while gaining rapport and to gain a clear picture of submodalities. If you really dig into most NLP patterns, they all use some form of anchoring in line with submodalities.

I am fortunate to have hundreds of success stores. But recently, I had a client, who we will call Sue, who was having a horrible time dealing with the fact that her life companion was dying from cancer. He was pushing her away during this time, and she had feelings of guilt, which in turn brought up feelings of inadequacy and abandonment, which she developed from past experiences. She was at a point of no longer going to work, getting dressed, or taking care of her personal health. She felt worthless, powerless, and undeserving of happiness. After only two sessions with both NLP and hypnosis, she was once again — according to herself and friends that came to meet me — a vivacious, confident, and happy woman. She could have empathy for her companion without the negative feelings and figured out herself that pushing her away was his way of trying to protect her from the results of this horrible ordeal. We also succeeded in placing the old experiences in her "mental library" for her to use as references to help protect her from reliving the same issues in her present and future life, preventing these negative experiences to impact her emotions or actions again.

Anyone seeking change in any aspect can improve his or her quality of life personally or professionally with NLP. If you get the opportunity to learn from the creator of the method or someone trained by him or her, I would say that would be your best bet. With that said, anyone can learn and apply the principles, but it does take practice to master.

Bandler's or Grinder's books and seminars seem to dominate the NLP training scene, and there is a lot of information on the Web. But beware — a lot of trash appears there as well. If you can, joining a group with others who are interested in learning and or practicing NLP is a good place to start.

Science does not support a multitude of subjects and practices. That does not mean they do not work or are not real. The simple answer is that I can prove it works to help a person change a belief or behavior because I have seen positive results with my clients. The opportunities are endless for NLP and hypnosis to have a powerful and positive impact in our world today to help us all lead a better quality of life. Above all else, you can never allow others to set their limitations on you.

Chapter 7

ANCHORING

Have you ever known someone who said they got angry because they just could not help it? Sometimes it does feel like your emotions and feelings are in charge, and you are helpless to stop them from taking over. NLP offers a way to immediately access a more resourceful state when you deal with unwanted feelings. You can access or return to a more useful state with anchoring.

Anchors and Future Pacing

Anchors are one of the most powerful tools of NLP. Anchors provide immediate access to the most useful and appropriate state for the moment. Future pacing allows anchor users to practice being in that useful state so it feels familiar.

The following section includes a discussion of anchors and future pacing and how to use both.

Positive anchors

Positive anchors work by associating a stimulus, such as an action, sound, or symbol, with a desired state. The symbol or action becomes the stimulus for moving into the desired state. In other words, the symbol or action leads to the state in much the same way that flipping a switch leads to a light-filled room. Here is another example: If every time you hear the music of Deuter you feel relaxed, the music and the feeling of being relaxed become associated. The music of Deuter serves as the anchor for the state of relaxation. Choosing to turn on the music is referred to in NLP as firing the anchor. If you begin to feel relaxed after you fire the anchor, you are said to have triggered the state. In the beginning, you may turn on Deuter because you heard from a friend that he or she finds the music soothing and relaxing. Or maybe you happened upon the music just before you drifted off to sleep one evening. At this stage, you are consciously aware of your desire to move into a relaxed state. With time, as the association between Deuter and feeling relaxed grows stronger, you will find your subconscious mind takes over. Each time you hear the music, any tension you feel in your body will melt away, your breathing will probably slow, and feelings of stress will begin to fade. The state of relaxation will begin to fill you automatically with no conscious thought required.

You can use any anchor you feel comfortable with. In fact, you probably already have experience with several anchors you have never even thought about before. Do you and your spouse or partner have a special song? Think about how you feel each time you hear the song. Without your even realizing it, the song has likely become an anchor for a state, such as romance. Or think of the emotional and physical response you have each time you smell a pie baking or Thanksgiving dinner on the stove. The stimuli or the smell of the food becomes the anchor, which evokes a predictable physical or emotional response. In the case of Thanksgiving dinner or the pie baking, even the memory can trigger feelings of warmth, family, comfort, and celebration.

The key for establishing a positive anchor is to create a strong association between the desired state and the stimulus or the anchor. In this way, you trigger the state or reach the desired state automatically, without even thinking about it. Anchoring is useful for triggering states or feelings or confidence, calmness, and even happiness. Once the association has been set, the desired state follows.

There are many instances in your daily life when you respond to both conscious and subconscious anchors. Ideally, you can set up anchors that help to achieve excellence, regardless of the setting. The best way to do this is to determine what state would be most useful in a particular situation. Consider the following:

What would be the best state to be in for:

- A job interview

- Delivering a presentation

- Teaching a class

- Reading a bedtime story to a child

- Running a marathon

- Participating in a parent teacher conference

- Asking for a raise

You are more likely to care your best self or most resourceful state into any circumstance when you take the time to understand what resources the circumstance will require. This will be discussed more later in the chapter.

Negative anchors

Because you understand the value of being able to get into the most resourceful state for any given circumstance, it is useful to know how you respond to various stimuli. When an anchor triggers a state that is not good for your current circumstance, you can consider it a negative anchor.

Sometimes the anchor or stimulus triggers a non-resourceful or undesirable state. For example, many people fear needles and avoid visiting doctors or dentists for this reason. Another example: Combat veterans often speak of the extreme anxiety they experience each time they hear loud noise or noises that remind them of gunfire. During combat, it was useful to be anxious and alert upon hearing loud or potentially dangerous noises. Outside the context of combat, that response is not necessarily useful. Thus, the stimulus, loud noise, is a negative anchor. Just as anchors are created by associating an experience with a stimulus, they can be extinguished by disassociating the stimulus from the experience.

Anchors can also be uncomfortable. Sometimes, these kinds of anchors can be used to manage behavior. Any parent who has ever given his or her child "the look" knows about uncomfortable anchors. A misbehaving child is quickly persuaded to behave just by seeing the look, which he or she associates with a consequence that is best avoided. Starting about 2007, large numbers of people experienced the uncomfortable anchor of the hearing the telephone ring or receiving mail. During this turbulent economic time, when so many people experienced unemployment and reduced income, a telephone ringing quickly became associated with harassing creditors and mail with fear of foreclosure or garnishment, both firing a state of extreme panic, helplessness, and anxiety.

Just as anchors are created, they can be broken. The process of breaking an anchor is called collapsing anchors, which will be discussed later in this chapter.

External stimuli that evoke an internal response

You can establish anchors with or without permission from your conscious mind. In the earlier example of the special song, the anchor was likely set in your subconscious mind. You were not even aware the anchor was being established. After all, you were likely too busy enjoying the company of your loved one to stop and say to yourself, "I am going to associate good feelings with this song, and every time I hear this song I will experience feelings of love, romance, and happiness." The same is true of the pie baking. The experiences and feelings that become associated with the pie will become evident each time you smell the pie baking.

It can help to think of an anchor as a conditioned response. The most well-known example of a conditioned response involves Pavlov. Born in 1849, Ivan Pavlov, a Russian psychologist, conducted a number of experiments during which he discovered that dogs would begin to salivate each time they encountered a stimulus they associated with food. Most famously, Pavlov's dogs are said to have salivated at the sound of a bell. Less known is that Pavlov studied a number of stimuli. In fact, it is even documented that the dogs began to salivate when they saw lab technicians in their typical garb of white lab jackets. Because the lab technicians fed the dogs, they began to associate the techs with eating and would salivate just with the sight of them.

The example of Pavlov's dogs should make clear that virtually anything can become an anchor. The power of the anchor is not simply in the stimulus, it is in the close association between the stimulus and the experience. Like dogs, human beings respond. Your experience of the environment is constantly imprinting on your memories and expectations. For example, most people are more likely to choose a package of chicken noodle soup that pictures a grandmother type proffering a steaming bowl of soup than they are to choose one labeled only with the words "chicken noodle soup." The package picturing the grandmother leads the buyer to assume, either consciously or unconsciously, that the soup will be better because it is associated with grandma's soup lovingly made or at least lovingly served. Even buyers who have not had such an experience of grandma serving them chicken noodle soup understand and are persuaded by the association. Consciously and unconsciously, you are always establishing behavior patterns and actions based on the world around you. Understanding anchors can help you plan external stimuli to evoke a particular desired response.

Link a positive state to a past occasion and relive it to set it

If you have ever run a 5K or a marathon, delivered a winning presentation, or successfully completed a project, then you are familiar with the resource state. A resource state is a positive, proactive, potential-filled experience. Future pacing allows you to connect resource states to cues in your future so that when needed, you can trigger them to help you achieve the best state for the circumstance. Go back to the list created earlier. The list contained several scenarios for which it would be helpful to determine the most useful state in advance. Now, look at two of these scenarios —

delivering a presentation and reading a bedtime story to a child. When delivering a presentation, the most useful state would likely include feeling prepared, confident, and relaxed. If you are reading a bedtime story to a child, the best state might be feeling goofy, patient, relaxed, or warm. You can create these feelings or any feeling you need for any situation by linking to a positive state from a past occasion and reliving it to set it. NLP uses an acronym for the process of setting anchors. The easy to remember acronym is RACE.

The following example illustrates two important ways to use anchors. First, to maintain patience during the often frustrating drive with chatty children in the back seat. An anchor would also be helpful here because even though the experience of having chatty children in the backseat can be frustrating, it can also be one of those ordinary extraordinary moments of life to look back on with warmth and fondness.

Using Anchors with Parenting

One of the best things about the lazy days of summer is the leisurely mornings. During the school year, we have to be ready for the arrival of the school bus at 6:56. Summer break means there is no bus. Instead, I drive my son to camp each morning before I head off to work.

Mind you there is a tradeoff. Where formerly I rode accompanied only by my thoughts and the music of my choice, I now have a very chatty companion. The Wiggles are his traveling music companions of choice.

I do not have enough fingers and toes to count how many times I hear the excited cry, "look," during our 30-minute ride. No, we do not take different paths. We travel the same way every day. Still, my son finds something new to delight him every, single time.

It does not matter how many times I say, "Mommy cannot turn around because she is driving." His excitement will not be reined in by mere safety concerns. It bubbles out of him. When I do turn around at a red light or stop sign, his eyes are as bright as they would be if 100-watt bulbs sat behind them.

He really sees the world — the sun shining through the trees, birds with wide wingspans soaring above, fire trucks, orange cars, and people walking dogs.

What does this all mean? I have to pay attention because he wants me to see all these things, too. Not as familiar objects though but as things unique to that moment. I am forced, then, to regard each thing anew — to look for the extraordinary in the seemingly ordinary.

I have heard it said that you never step in the same river twice because it constantly flows and changes. These car rides remind me that life is also ever changing. Every day is brand new. Sometimes while rushing here and there, too busy even to stop for gas, we fail to notice. Sometimes we behave as if we are living the same day over and over again. We imagine ourselves in a rut because we fail to experience instead of assume.

Assuming we have been there and done that, we do not experience people, places, or moments as we could. For example, we do not listen because we think we already know; we do not look because we think we have seen it all before; and we do not stay present because we assume the moment before or after this one is, for one reason or another, more important.

Tomorrow we will head out for camp. I cannot guess what will grab my son's attention along the way, but whatever it is, I am looking forward to hearing about it.

Creating Positive Anchors

Use the RACE method to enter into the most useful state for delivering a presentation.

Public speaking is among the top five fears for most people. The very idea causes many people to break out in a cold sweat. Obviously, this is not the most useful state to achieve excellence in presentations. Remember that NLP mantra, if anyone can do it — in this case deliver a winning presentation — then anyone can learn to do it. RACE shows you how to create a positive anchor.

Relive — Perhaps you do not yet feel confident about public speaking. Chances are you have experienced feelings of confidence in another setting. The first step in setting an anchor is to relive or recall as vividly as possible a past experience where you felt confident.

Go to a place where you are not likely to be distracted or interrupted; you will need several minutes to fully focus on the recall experience. As you recall the experience of feeling confident, use each of the submodalities. Remember that refer to your sensory modalities or the senses you use to interpret information about the world around you. These five sense modes — visual (sight), auditory (sound), kinesthetic (feeling), olfactory (smell), and gustatory (taste) — can be fine tuned to make the recall experience seem more vivid and real. Think now of a past experience where you felt confident. What did you see? Fine tune your visual modality by making the colors as sharp and bright as you can. When creating an anchor, it is best to use as many of the as you can to enhance the feeling of actually being in that place and time. Engage each of your senses as you relive the experience. What did you hear, feel, smell, and taste? Again, turn the volume up on each of those sensory memories. Reliving is the closest thing we have to time travel or "do-overs." The internal experience of the event in memory should be created so vividly that it matches the physical experience in reality. Reliving positive experiences allows you to harness the useful feelings produced to fuel additional excellent experiences. What if you cannot remember ever having the feeling or experience you want to anchor? You can still set the anchor by imagining that you had the experience. Even if the memory is not your own, you have likely experienced the feeling through a friend or even through a character in a book or movie.

Anchor. As you experience feeling confident, you must associate a stimulus or anchor with this state. Associating a stimulus or anchoring the state allows you to access and use the good feelings from this state to create the same state whenever you need it. Choose any anchor you like.

Many successful anchors are set with different parts of the body — normally the hands — so they are always accessible and ready to be fired. Folding the hands together is an anchor that has been previously mentioned in this book. Other body anchors might include positioning or crossing the fingers in certain way. The key is to choose an anchor that feels right for you and one you are likely to use. Strengthen your anchor by using more than one. Think of your primary representational mode. Remember that the sense or representational modes are visual, auditory, kinesthetic, olfactory, and gustatory. If you consider yourself to be an auditory person, an auditory anchor may be best for you. For example, as you fold your hands together, you might also say something to yourself like, "I feel confident" or "Delivering presentations is really easy for me." You might even associate feelings of confidence with a particular sound in much the same way that a gong can evoke a meditative state.

Change or create a distraction. In the third step of creating an anchor, you should break state. As soon as the anchor is set, seek out a distraction that takes you out of the state for which you have set the anchor. Breaking state can be as simple as changing your train of thought. Instead of reliving the experience you are using to set the anchor, you can switch your thoughts to what you will have for dinner or your schedule for the next several days. The key is to remove yourself from the state you are anchoring.

Evoke or test your anchor. The final step in creating an anchor is the test. Because you broke state in step three, it will be easy for you to notice as you test or fire your anchor whether you have actually triggered the state. Assume that folding your hands is the anchor. After you have spent a few minutes reviewing your schedule for next week, fold your hands to evoke feelings of confidence. Creating anchors often works the first time through the RACE steps. If after you have gone through each of the steps you are unable to evoke the desired response, do not worry. Run through each of the steps again, giving particular attention to each of the modalities. You should be fully in the experience as if it is happening in the moment. Creating strong anchors is most successful when you set the anchor during the most intense part of the relived experience. You can repeat the four steps of creating an anchor with many different positive experiences to improve your chances of reliably evoking the desired response. In NLP, the process of repeating these steps with many positive experiences is known as stacking anchors.

Feeling confident is only one of the many ways that anchors can help you access useful states. Anchoring can also help with the earlier example of reading a bedtime story to a child. With such time crunched schedules and work pressures, it can sometimes be difficult to let go of stress, tension, and anxiety and relax with a bedtime story. You can learn to immediately shift from harried mode to a relaxed state by creating an anchor. Once the anchor is set, story time becomes a pleasant respite in a whirlwind day instead of one more chore to check off a list.

Resource — an anchor that genuinely provides good feelings

Remember the presupposition "People have all the resources they need"? Anchors help you immediately access any internal resource you need in a given moment. Imagine being plagued by a feeling of anxiety. Chances are anxiety is only one of the many feelings you have experienced in your life. You have also likely experienced calm and confidence. Anchoring allows you to access the feeling of calm if it is more appropriate than anxiety for the situation at hand.

Collapsing — a process for breaking negative anchors

This book previously discussed negative anchors. An anchor or stimulus, whether positive or negative, generates a physiological response. Like positive anchors, negative anchors can be set during any experience that creates an association. When that response is not useful for where you are or what you are trying to accomplish, you can break the anchor. Breaking the anchor is also called collapsing the anchor. *The following exercise includes the steps for collapsing anchors.*

Exercise 10: Collapsing Anchors

If a particular anchor evokes an unwanted state, NLP can help you remove that anchor and create a positive one that triggers a more useful state. Collapsing, neutralizing, or extinguishing anchors works by triggering opposing states — positive and negative — simultaneously. Ideally, the positive state, which is stronger, wins over the negative one, causing it to be neutralized.

Step 1: Determine which state you want to break. For example, if every time you hear the word "jump" you feel afraid, the state you want to break is fear. You want to break the association between hearing the word jump and your response of fear that the word elicits.

Step 2: Decide how you want to feel instead. For example, you may decide that each time you hear the word jump, you want to feel relaxed or happy instead of fear.

Step 3: Create a positive anchor using the steps learned with RACE. Relive the positive experience associated with the way you want to feel when you hear the word jump. Anchor the feeling using one or more stimuli, such as a hand position and a word or phrase you say to yourself. Change your thoughts; break the state by allowing your mind to be occupied by a completely different train of thought. Evoke the desired feeling by firing the anchor or anchors you have chosen to trigger the state.

Step 4: It is important that you remember to break state after you create the anchor for the positive feelings you want to trigger. After you break state, you will then create an anchor for the negative state, again using the steps learned with RACE. Also, remember to test your anchor to be sure it evokes the desired response. In this case, you should have two anchors for two responses: The feeling you want to have — relaxed or happy — and the feeling you do not want to have — fear.

Step 5: Break state again by distracting yourself with unrelated thoughts, such as who won last week's ballgame or what Apple® will come up with next.

Step 6: Fire both the positive and the negative anchors in succession. Do not break state between firing the opposing anchors. After two or three rounds, fire both anchors simultaneously. Break the anchor associated with the negative state while maintaining the anchor associated with the positive state.

Step 7: Test again by firing the negative anchor. If you have collapsed the anchor, you will not evoke the fear response, or maybe what you experience will be a reduced fear response. You may even feel no response and feel completely neutral in response to the anchor previously associated with fear. If you still experience unwanted feelings, you can repeat the RACE steps and or combine anchors. For example, pair a hand position — crossed fingers — with a word — carefree — or a word with a sound — water — or an object — a smooth stone you hold — with a word.

Using Anchors Effectively

There are three important points to remember about anchors:

1. The anchor should be set right at or just a few seconds before the most intense or peak portion of the recall experience. For example, if you are anchoring confidence to finish a race, you would begin by reliving another race you completed successfully. Set your anchor just before you cross the finish line and hold it until just after you cross the finish line in your mind. In this way, you capture the most intense feelings to which you will associate your anchor. Remember to interrupt or break state just after you cross the finish line so you anchor only the wanted feeling — confidence to finish the race and not an unintended feeling, such as tired or worried about an injury after the race.

2. The anchor should be unique. Avoid an anchor you commonly use. For example, if your anchor is crossed fingers, take care that you only use cross fingers to trigger that state and not under other circumstances.

3. Finally, your anchor should be consistent so it is firmly and reliably established. Each and every time you want to trigger the state of confidence in races, fire the trigger in exactly the same way.

Another way to use anchors effectively is with future pacing. Whether you are trying to firmly established a positive anchor or are trying to strengthen a positive anchor that has "won out" over a negative one that has been neutralized, you can future pace to improve results. Here is a look at future pacing after an anchor has been successfully extinguished.

Jimmy hates doing homework. His mom is going to work with him on establishing new behavior by creating an anchor for him. Mom begins by asking Jimmy to remember a time when he really did not want to do his homework. She can help him recreate the experience by asking him specific questions about the memory. This process is called eliciting. Eliciting is just a short way of saying that she helped uncover what was happening for Jimmy internally by asking him questions. Questions Jimmy's mom might ask include: What were you thinking? How where you feeling? What did you see and/or hear? As Jimmy answers the questions, his mother watches him and listens to him for clues that he has fully stepped into the memory. Jimmy's mom uses calibration to interpret his body language and nonverbal responses.

Calibration is simply learning to interpret what another person thinks and feels using nonverbal cues as a guide. Jimmy's mother notes his body language and facial cues as they begin to discuss the problem behavior. She uses that information as a baseline for measuring distance between the problem state, not doing homework, and the desired state, doing homework. In the problem state, Jimmy might look defeated, embarrassed, and anxious. His mom could determine this based on his tone of voice, his coloring, posture, breathing, and even where he directs his gaze. After the anchor has been established and new behavior set, Jimmy's mom is likely to see different clues that signal the change.

When Jimmy is most deeply engaged in the relived experience, his mother sets an auditory and visual anchor. Next, mom asks Jimmy to remember a time when he felt excited to do his homework. She asks the same questions and again sets one or two anchors.

After the anchors have been set, Jimmy's mother interrupts his state with a distraction. When mom is sure Jimmy has broken state, she fires both anchors in rapid succession and then simultaneously. Ideally, the negative anchor will be extinguished and the positive anchor will be set. Mom reinforces the positive anchor with future pacing. She now invites Jimmy to engage in a future memory of himself eagerly completing his homework. Again, Jimmy is encouraged to make the experience as vivid as possible.

As discussed earlier, anchors can be established consciously or subconsciously. Anchors can also be set by individuals and with others. To use anchors most effectively, it is important to understand how you respond to the many types of stimuli you experience. How you experience stimuli often depends on the strength of the association and, in some cases, the setting in which the stimuli is present. For example, how you respond to a certain stimulus at a party might be different from the way you would respond in a place of worship. Using anchors effectively requires some knowledge of how and when you respond to stimuli and knowing when a response should be encouraged or extinguished.

Eliciting and calibrating — evoking a feeling and identifying the associated behavior and language

It is also possible to set anchors in others through eliciting and calibrating. Eliciting uses questions to reveal the internal processes of another person. In the earlier example of future pacing, Jimmy's mother used eliciting to help him represent his experience of not wanting to do homework. She also used eliciting to help him represent the desired state of wanting to do homework. Asking questions that help a person get into state is called eliciting. Eliciting is one of four major steps for setting an anchor with others. The other most important steps for setting an anchor with others are: create rapport, calibrate, and test. The following is an example.

Pat would like to establish an anchor for relaxation in a new hire she is training. She knows the employee feels a little nervous and worries his anxiety will interfere with his ability to grasp the information she is sharing. Pat begins by building rapport. You will recall that building rapport is a way of connecting with someone else by communicating with a sense of familiarity. There are several ways to create rapport by understanding and matching the other person's primary representational system with your own verbal and nonverbal language. For example, Pat notices right away that the new hire has a kinesthetic representational system. She chooses phrases like "tackle the training" and "get your hands on the project" when talking about the training.

Pat helps the new hire get into a relaxed state with eliciting. She uses questions to help him remember a time when he felt relaxed. Because Pat understands the importance of calibration, she notices how the new hire looks when he is in his non-resourceful state — i.e. anxious — so she can visually observe his shift after the useful state has been established. For example, Pat might observe the new hire drop his shoulders, relax his breathing, and soften, slow, or lower his voice.

When Pat sees the new hire is experiencing the height of his relaxation memory, she sets an anchor. She might tap a pen or tilt her head at a particular angle. Pat then disrupts the state by introducing a distracting thought. Pat then fires the anchor to see if she has triggered the state. She uses her earlier cues from calibration to test if she has successfully set the anchor.

Using the TOTE model to check your progress

The TOTE model — Test, Operate, Test, Exit — is a basic strategy for checking progress with anything you do. For example, you can use the TOTE model to test the association between your anchor and desired state, and you can use it to check if you have successfully set an anchor or created rapport with another person. TOTE works like this — test to be sure you get the result you want, operate or tweak what you do if you do not get the results you want, test again to see if you now get the results you want, and exit — when you get the result you want or decide to stop trying for the result.

When setting an anchor, it can help to gauge the intensity of the feeling you trigger on a scale of one to ten, with ten being the most intense. Successful anchors trigger the most intense feelings. If your anchor does not consistently trigger the intended resource state, avoid firing it. Firing an anchor meant to trigger confidence that instead triggers anxiety because it is not working is self-defeating.

Altering states with anchors

Anchors help you organize your internal resources against the capricious nature of external stimuli. If at any time external stimuli trigger a negative state, it is possible to alter that state with anchors. Altering states helps you access the resources needed for the situation at hand.

Altering your state is much like changing the direction you are headed in with your car. Here is an example: You are driving down the road, and while you are at a stop light, the car in the next lane says your tire looks flat. Instead of continuing straight, you turn left into the garage on the corner. You had a problem, and rather than continue driving on a soon-to-be-flat tire, you immediately accessed the readily available resource of the garage to move out of the problem state, flat tire, into a desired state, good tire.

Here is how altering states might look in your external and internal world. You have heard often you are not the most patient person around. You gather this feedback is accurate because you have heard it often in your personal and your professional life. Being patient has become particularly important lately because it is the foundation of your plan to improve your parenting. You have set an auditory anchor, the word "calm," and a visual anchor, ocean waves. Because you understand it is within your power to control what you think, how you feel, and what you do, you decide that each time you find yourself approaching the unwanted state — impatience — you will fire your anchors. In that way, you come to have control of yourself based on what happens within you rather than what happens around you. In other words, you harness your resources to alter unwanted states rather than allow yourself to be thrown into and remain in those unwanted states.

Anchors offer a powerful way to employ your best resources in service to your goal of excellence. It does not matter what problem state you try to change into a desired state; the change is always possible. Improve your chances of success with anchors by using as many of your sense modes as you can as you relive the positive experience. Set your anchor at the peak of the relived experience. Consider using multiple anchors, such as pairing an auditory and visual anchor. Remember that stacking several positive experiences on the same anchor can strengthen the anchor.

Finally, do not forget future pacing. Vividly see and feel yourself experiencing the desired state.

Anchors help you exercise control over your thoughts and feelings. Anchors also eliminate the paralysis and loss of control that often results from negative thoughts and feelings. Use anchors to access any resourceful feeling you might need in a given circumstance. Even if you have never experienced the feeling, the ability to create an anchor is still available to you. Simply use an experience you read or heard about. You will quickly find that many of the roadblocks in your life that seemed insurmountable will begin to shrink. This is because, as you know, people have all the resources they need. Anchors help you quickly access those resources and apply them for the best outcomes.

Chapter 8

SUBMODALITIES

S ubmodalities allow you to master your representation of anything by using your senses to deepen color, add depth, enrich sound, or enlarge the picture. Using your senses to fine tune your inner representation of memories and events makes it possible to turn up the feelings and pictures — as with desirable experiences — or turn them down — as with undesirable experiences.

Fine Tuning Modalities (Representational Systems)

The representational system is also referred to in NLP as the sensory modalities. These are visual or sight, auditory or sound, kinesthetic or feeling (both emotion and tactile), olfactory or smell, and gustatory or taste. The sense modes are also called the representational system because you use each of your senses to develop an internal representation of your memories and ideas.

Think of a memory you have. It is your senses that make it possible for you to experience that memory. You see what happened, you remember how it felt and what you heard, you can even recall scents associated with what happened. Memories are more vivid when you can reproduce clear, sharp sensory representations of events. The difference between creating an appealing internal representation and one that does not make much of an impression is much like watching a movie on two different television screens. One screen is 60 inches and includes a high-definition picture and stereo surround sound. The other screen is 9 inches, with poor sound quality and in fuzzy black and white. Put another way, the difference is much the same as watching a concert in an amphitheater in the front row or in the farthest balcony where you will need to use binoculars. Vivid representations are more like actually being there or re-experiencing the event than fuzzy or dull representations.

Finer distinctions of senses (visual, auditory, kinesthetic)

You use your senses to interpret, understand, and communicate about the world around you. When you think about it, it is impossible to talk about an idea, memory, or experience without involving your senses. Without using your senses, how could you describe your day at work, your favorite meal, or a loved one's smile? Even if you did not use language, but instead thought about each of those things, your senses would still be involved. You might see in your mind the exact angle of your loved one's head or the light in his or her eyes as he or she smiled. You might feel how excited or frustrated you are about the project you are working on at work. You might smell your favorite meal and recall the complex tastes of the deeply flavored dish. Consider the following exercise.

EXERCISE 11: EMPLOYING SENSE MODES

Although the representational system is always at work, it is rarely given much conscious thought. Rarely do we tie our ability to vividly experience an event internally to our motivation for creating that event externally. The following exercise highlights the difference in feeling between a vivid, strongly recalled event and one that has little or no meaning.

Step 1: Think about a key memory or experience in your life. The memory should be a strong one, such as the day you got married, the day your child was born, or the day of another momentous occasion.

Step 2: Write about the event in as much detail as possible. Notice how you feel as you write. Notice how many senses you use to describe the memory.

Step 3: Now think about an event that does not hold much significance for you. Write about the event in as much detail as possible. Notice how you feel as you write and how many senses you use to describe the memory.

Step 4: Compare the two written pieces. Chances are you could write much more and in greater detail about the key memory. As you wrote about your key memory, you probably also felt many of the same feelings you experienced in that moment. It may have seemed almost as if you were transported back in time. Your memories of the event that held little significance for you were probably difficult to grasp. You may have even been unsure about what you saw, felt, or heard and found it difficult to clearly retrieve the memory.

Think again about your key memory. If you wrote about something like your marriage or the birth of a child, the strong feelings you experienced as you wrote probably stayed with you. You may have even acted on those feelings and given your spouse or child a hug or called to say, "I love you."

Reliving an experience vividly can enrich and empower you by giving you access to the exact feelings you had in that moment. That is why the representational system is such an important tool for achieving goals, staying in your most resourceful state, and communicating well.

Your representational system gives meaning to each of your experiences. There is no way to represent an experience or idea without your sense modes. The representational system can also be important for achieving desired outcomes. The beginning of this chapter mentioned the difference between watching a movie on a 60-inch screen versus a 9-inch screen.

Watching on the 60-inch screen is much like being there, while the 9-inch screen makes the events that are happening seem distant and very far away.

One of the strategies for achieving outcomes involves first vividly representing the experience of the outcome in your mind. If the experience is represented so clearly it feels like it has already happened, your motivation to achieve the outcome grows stronger. At the same time, your clear internal representation of the event reduces any resistance you may have felt about achieving the outcome.

Internal representations of desired events should be as bold and compelling as possible. These mind pictures should feel almost as if you could step into or reach out and grab them. In other words, because these pictures feel so real, you can easily associate into them. Associating into the memory or created experience helps you think, act, and feel as if the event is happening. Desired events and feelings should be viewed in the mind's eye on that 60-inch screen so they are easily associated into. Undesired events and feelings should be viewed on the 9-inch screen so they are easily disassociated from.

Fine tuning modalities is much like adjusting the contrast, brightness, and sound buttons on your television. It is also like sitting close to the television versus sitting 12 feet away from it or the difference between smelling a freshly cut lemon and a lemon drink made from concentrate. Here are some examples of how each of the sense modes can be adjusted for optimal fine tuning.

Visual submodalities may include brightness or color

Think about the last time you saw a commercial for a hamburger. The hamburger commercial likely showed a close-up picture of juicy, richly browned patties, purple onions, and bright red tomatoes. You may have even seen someone swooning over the first generous bite. A picture of the competing burger would have been shown as smaller, in black and white, and not so close-up. The commercial was no accident. It was planned to create interest in the advertised burger by making the picture as inviting and vivid as possible.

It is possible to visually create the same kinds of pictures internally. Pictures in the mind's eye can be made more compelling with adjustments to the size and proximity. Images can also be sharpened or brightened with vivid color and attention to detail. For example, when picturing the bedroom of your dream home, see the color of the walls, the furniture, and books in the room, and even the trees or flowers outside the bedroom windows.

Giving attention to the visual modality means the difference between a clear color photo and one that has cracked and faded with age. In the first photo, the entire picture and every detail it captures can be clearly seen. In the second photo, it is unclear what might have been captured by the photo because the details are unclear. Practice manipulating the visual modality by picturing the last really great day you shared with a friend or loved one. Write down or describe to him or her everything you see. Now, ask him or her to describe what he or she saw. How do the pictures compare?

Auditory submodalities may include pitch or volume

Remember hearing a soft drink commercial at the height of summer. You probably remember the sound of ice cubes clinking in the glass, the sound of the fizzy drink being poured over the ice cubes, and finally a refreshed sounding "ahhhh." You probably also heard words like ice cold, refreshing, and thirst quenching. Each of the words and sounds was designed to create appeal and interest in the drink. On hearing the sounds, many listeners probably imagined themselves enjoying an ice-cold drink and felt a sudden desire to enjoy the advertised drink because familiar sounds were associated with the pleasant experience of enjoying a cold drink on a hot summer day. Stepping into that remembered experience, assuming it was positive, created a desire to actually have the experience.

You need not be an advertiser to successfully fine tune the auditory modality. Practice now with your favorite song, ocean waves, or chirping birds. Hear the sounds first at high and then low volume. Now, close and far away; change the pitch as you continue listening. Introduce a competing sound or imagine the sound is muffled. How did your experience of the sound change with fine tuning?

Kinesthetic submodalities may include texture or emotion

If you have ever experienced or heard someone talk about receiving bad news and feeling as if he or she had been punched in the gut, you already understand the feeling sense. The kinesthetic modality concerns feelings; the kind you experience emotionally and through touch. Spend a few moments recalling a time you felt joyful, proud, and angry. Where in your body did you experience each feeling? How would you describe the feeling if you had to use words, pictures, or sounds? What thoughts are associated with your feelings? It is not uncommon to be able to access very strong feelings about an event long after the event is over. For example, either you or someone you know can easily access as much rage about an event today as was felt in the moment. Each time it comes up, his or her breathing accelerates, the voice may become louder and more agitated, and there are likely to be changes in body tension, facial coloring, and expression.

Managing or fine tuning the kinesthetic modality gives you the tools to turn up good feelings and turn down bad ones. Think about the old angry feelings. The feelings are likely still fresh because the image or representation of the event is still very vivid in the mind. To detach or disassociate from the feelings about the event, it is important to blur, darken, or otherwise turn down any internal representations of the event. Consider again the sounds associated with the anger-producing event. Say the dominant image is someone yelling at you or maybe even the crash of an object thrown in your direction. You can change the sound by softening it or distort it by switching the angry voice to the voice of Alvin the Chipmunk. If the image is an angry face, you can distort or blur the face by making it fuzzy and far away so it is not so close and disturbing. Likewise, to enjoy more of the good feelings experienced in a past event, you need only turn up your representations of that event.

Now, think about a time you felt very cold or very hot. Remember a time when you felt physical pain. Thinking of a time when you were cold, you might feel how much your fingers or toes hurt. Now, imagine being held or touched by a loved one. You can make the memory more real by recalling how he or she smelled, the texture of the skin or clothing, and the firmness or lightness of touch. The memory, well crafted, can be calming and soothing. Again, fine tuning modalities gives you immediate access to your most resourceful state. You can create a clear internal representation of an experience just by maximizing your sense modes; the feelings associated with that experience are now yours to enjoy.

Using the Swish Pattern to Make Behavioral Changes

People have all the resources they need. The Swish pattern is another NLP strategy for providing access to those resources. This easy-to-use pattern can immediately result in positive behavioral changes and improved self-esteem. Making these changes is as simple as creating a future self who has already dealt with the problem or feeling. The future self-image is super imposed on the less resourceful current image until the latter image disappears.

Exposure to the future self builds self-esteem because it improves how you think about yourself and what you are able to do. Because the future self has already conquered whatever problem you are dealing with, you begin to feel more confident in the moment to handle the situation. It is also true that success begets success. As you prove your future self right by tackling formerly problem situations, your confidence and success in any difficult situation will grow.

You can use the Swish pattern for any number of problems, such as fear of public speaking, anger, low motivation, and feeling confident. In fact, you can use the pattern in virtually any situation where you want to transform current behavior. Visually speaking, the Swish pattern might look like an interior decorator's portfolio. In the first picture, you can see things as they are — a room that is perhaps functional but needs upgrades for its current use. In the second picture, you see the room improved and transformed. The room has been changed to accommodate current needs and functions. You are always growing and evolving. As you encounter different situations, you may need different skills to be successful in the settings. The Swish pattern can help you build those skills, as well as discard old behaviors that no longer serve you.

Rapid submodality shifts associate two mental images

The more attractive and real the picture, the more motivation there is to achieve or attain the internally created state externally. Also, there is a lot of value in creating unattractive pictures of unwanted states. Creating a dull, unattractive picture of an unwanted state makes it seem far away and unappealing when compared with the positive picture. The Swish pattern is an extension of this idea.

The Swish pattern process looks much like a before and after picture. Your before picture shows everything about what symbolizes the problem situation. For example, if you have a fear of public speaking, your before picture might show an audience of people laughing or sleeping through your speech. You might also see yourself stumbling over words, tripping, or sweating profusely. You can even feel your heart racing as you agonize over a frozen PowerPoint® presentation. In other words, you see a disaster. The Swish pattern lets you trade the before picture, the one you do not want, for an after picture, the scenario you really do want.

The after picture is completely different. This is your idea of the presentation exactly as it could be with more feelings of confidence. Your after picture allows you to safely create a vivid picture of yourself as someone who has already handled and overcome the problem. This is your chance to be you but improved. This does not mean you suddenly become the kind of presenter who keeps the audience laughing if that is not who you are. It does mean you bring your best authentic self — the person you are when doubt, fear, and insecurity do not hold you back.

In your after photo, the audience is pictured as attentive and engaged. You are smiling, relaxed, and confident. In fact, you feel so confident that you no longer dread public speaking; it feels natural to you.

To make your own before picture you must first identify the trigger that initiates the undesired behavior. Following are a few examples:

New Feeling	Trigger
Anger	Being yelled at, feeling foolish, feeling disrespected, being tricked or lied to/about
Self-consciousness	Being criticized, being on the spot
Stress	Being rushed, unprepared, overwhelmed, late
Write about your feelings and triggers in the following columns:	

Now that you have had time to consider some of your triggers, choose a problem you would like to work on. *The following uses stress as an example.*

Linda feels stressed every time she feels rushed and unprepared. She begins to feel she will never be able to do everything she needs to do, and as a result, she spends so much time worrying that she gets done even less than she imagined. The problem affects her at work and at home. It seems she never has enough hours in the day, and residual tasks just seem to ratchet up her stress level even more. Her to-do list seems ever longer, while her feelings of accomplishment are almost nonexistent.

For her before picture, Linda sees herself looking flushed, rushed, harried, and small. She is surrounded by mountains of papers, dishes, laundry, and mail — unfinished tasks that loom over her. Linda must switch her focus from what is happening to what she wants to happen. Next, she must create her after picture. Linda begins by identifying the feelings she might attribute to someone who easily manages tasks at hand.

To make your own after picture, identify some of the feelings or behaviors of someone who has solved the problem you are dealing with. NLP provides a framework for modeling human excellence. So, remember that if a thing has been done — in this case managing tasks without being overcome by stress — then it can be done. The process begins with the realization that if someone else has more success in a particular area, it does not mean they are necessarily more capable than you are. Remember the presupposition, "People are not broken." What it does mean is they use their resources differently than you do at this time. You can also change the way you use your resources to achieve the same success. Creating the after picture helps you begin to do that.

For Linda and her problem of becoming overwhelmed by stress, she should make a list of behaviors and attitudes that she can use for creating and picturing her future self. Linda might call her future self "organized Linda" or "stressless Linda." This is how she might describe herself:

Stressless Linda:

- Is mindful of inner chatter. She consistently gives herself positive feedback about her ability to handle the tasks that come her way. Instead of telling herself, "I will never get all of this done," Linda says, "I am capable and confident I can complete these tasks."

- Practices self-care. She recognizes when she needs to take a deep breath and refocus her thoughts and energy on remaining in her most positive state.

- Has good boundaries. Linda challenges herself, but she is realistic about how much she can handle well. Linda knows the value of a saying no when she needs to.

- Is organized. Linda has taken a few hours to organize a system she thinks will help her manage tasks without wasted energy or effort.

- Manages her time well. Linda prepares her lunch and decides on her outfit the night before. She also goes to bed an hour earlier and gets up on time each morning so she does not feel rushed or tired.

- Has a realistic idea of how long the tasks she must complete actually take. Stressless Linda knows what stressed-out Linda did not — many tasks take far less time than you imagine they will.

- Knows when to delegate or ask for help.

- Breaks big tasks into smaller, more manageable steps.

- Makes leisure time a priority.

Now that Linda knows who she is as her future, stressless self, she can begin to create a visual picture to impose over her current picture of stressed-out Linda. In her after picture, Linda is composed. Where there once were mountainous tasks looming over her, there are now small, neat piles. Linda sees a to-do list with most of the items checked off and an hourglass showing she has plenty of time. The after picture shows a capable, less-stress Linda. Linda feels drawn to her future self and the desire to become the woman she pictures is strong.

Armed with a good picture of her desired outcome, Linda is ready to switch the pictures. First, she holds up the before picture. Then, Linda superimposes the after picture on top of the before picture. As the after picture settles into place, it grows larger and brighter. The after picture is being fine tuned with great attention to the visual modality. The picture continues developing and begins to look like it is three-dimensional. The colors are vivid, and everything pictured is sharp and clear. As Linda visualizes the picture, she thinks about her description of herself as stressless. She remembers stressless Linda's behaviors and attitudes and uses the words to encourage herself while focused on the picture. For example, Linda might say, "I am organized and capable" or "I have what it takes to complete even the biggest tasks" or "I always get things done." Linda will practice quickly moving the after picture onto the before picture several times until the change feels complete. This strategy is called the Swish pattern for the imagined sound the pictures makes as they move into place. Practice using any sound that is most effective for you as you switch your before and after pictures.

As mentioned earlier in this chapter, the Swish pattern can work for many problems, such as fear of public speaking or angry feelings. The Swish pattern can also help manage other problems, such as unwanted habits or food cravings.

Think about the last time you had a food craving. The craving was probably sharp and vivid. In fact, you could almost taste the thing you craved. Maybe you could even see and smell the food or imagine how you would feel as you took your first bite. As you vividly imagined this food, the desire to consume it actually consumed you. Even if it meant blowing your diet, you knew you had to have it.

A vividly imagined feeling or experience seems almost real. This kind of powerful visualization creates strong motivation to externalize or make real the imagined experience. The Swish pattern helps eliminate unwanted behaviors and food cravings by manipulating the picture to minimize attraction and desire. In other words, say the desired food is a bowl of cookies and cream ice cream. As you think about the ice cream, you see the chunks of cookie and imagine how they will feel as you chew them. You feel the cold creaminess of the ice cream on your tongue and imagine the slight chill you feel with the first bite. The bowl feels cold in your hands and the rich ice cream slides smoothly down your throat. The experience of eating that ice cream feels far more real than your desire to drop a pant size.

To manage a food craving, remember to turn down the volume on the unwanted visualization — in this case, the ice cream. Change the way you think about the ice cream so it appears less attractive and desirable. To understand the difference, think about eating something you do not have strong feelings about. The food item is probably not sharply represented in your mind, and you do not feel as if you could almost taste it.

As you turn down the volume on the unwanted picture, you must also turn up the volume on the wanted one — in this case, a smaller pant size. To do this, go through the steps used earlier to describe a person who has already solved the problem you are dealing with. What kinds of things does a person who manages his or her ideal weight do? How does a person who maintains his or her ideal weight think? What motivates a person who maintains his or her ideal weight? Which of these attitudes and behaviors can you adopt or model to create your own excellence with weight management?

For this switch, your before picture could show you eating the ice cream, being above your ideal weight, and holding onto self-defeating thoughts — however you imagine that might look. The after picture shows your future self. In this picture, you are at your ideal weight and have embraced the behaviors and attitudes of someone who maintains his or her ideal weight — however you imagine that might look. As before, hold the before picture up and quickly switch your after picture in front of it. Let your new picture first begin to overtake and finally obscure the old one. Remember to sharpen the new picture and to make it even more attractive and compelling as you hold it in your mind's eye. Make the switch several times until your desire for the ice cream is gone.

The Swish pattern can also help you successfully eliminate unwanted behavior or build motivation to complete a dreaded task. There are no limits to how you can use the pattern. As you use the Swish pattern to create excellence in your life, do not forget the importance of fine tuning submodalities.

The before picture — this is often you in a way you do not want to be regarding something you are thinking, feeling, or doing — should not be attractive or motivating. You create attraction or motivation through visualization by making the picture easy to associate with. It is more difficult to associate with or connect to a small fuzzy picture than it is to a large, bright one.

The after picture — this is a picture of the future you thinking, feeling, or doing something in the desired way — should be as clear and compelling as a movie. It should be easy to imagine yourself in the picture because it is so highly detailed. This picture is created with as many of your senses as possible. It uses strong visual detail, sound, feeling, and perhaps even taste and smell. The after picture provides strong motivation to create the imagined experience.

An often mentioned, presupposition of NLP is that people have all the resources they need. In any circumstance, that leaves you feeling non-resourceful, but you have only to determine what resources you need. You can then access those resources within yourself by using the Swish pattern. The Swish pattern simply lets you bring the needed resources to a place where you have not used them before. It does not matter how long you have struggled with the unwanted thought or behavior pattern. When you bring additional resources to the problem situation, you change your mental map. In other words, what you see as possible expands, while what you see as impossible fades or contracts. Because you have added to your mental map, there are new distances to reach and new turns to take. Additional resources provide access to greater territory and ultimately to the kind of success you want to create.

```
CASE STUDY:
JONATHAN ROYLE
ON THE MAGIC OF NLP
Jonathan Royle
The Mindcare Organisation Ltd
Hypnotic Consultant
The Mindcare Organisation Ltd,
c/o Prospect House Publishing,
Prospect House,
P.O. Box 12,
Huddersfield, England, HD8 9YP.
royle@magicalguru.com
www.magicalguru.com
Phone: 07050-377579
```

I was born plain Alex William Smith on Aug. 13, 1975, into a showbiz family while traveling with Gandey's Circus; I made my stage debut at age 3 as Flap the Clown. By 8, I performed a magic and illusion act. At 14, I was treating people with hypnotherapy and NLP and also doing stage hypnosis and mind-reading style shows.

I was originally taught hypnosis by two veteran UK hypnotists, Delavar and Brian Howard. I have earned money as a professional hypnotherapist for more than 21 years and as a stage and performance hypnotist for more than 20 years.

At age 8, I started reading books on psychology, hypnosis, and NLP. I quickly realized I was already using many of these techniques as a performer. The great comedians, magicians, and entertainers in general are all — usually without knowing it — masters of what we now commonly call NLP.

I presented my first training seminar to teach other hypnotists the techniques I had personally developed back in 1993 and have ran training seminars ever since. During that time, I taught my unique and proven techniques to doctors, nurses, plastic surgeons, and some of the world's most successful hypnotists and NLPers.

Over the years, I also helped organize and promote seminars for other leading names in the industry, and along the way, I have also benefited from training with them.

I have helped promote and/or organize seminars for and trained with Tom Silver (America's favorite television hypnotist), Nik and Eva Speakman (stars of "A Life Coach Less Ordinary"), Andrew Newton (the man who taught Paul McKenna), Richard Nongard and John Cerbone (creators of speed trance), Robert Phipps (UK television's body language expert), Barrie St. John (creator of hypno-sensory therapy), Paul Brady (creator of inner revision therapy), and Tom Bolton and Beverley Anderson (creators of the Freeway-Cer approach).

I work with people of all ages with all problems, and I truly believe that anything and everything is possible to achieve using hypnosis. In my opinion, hypnosis is where NLP comes from. As I teach in my training, it certainly works for the same reasons and more rapidly. In my experience, longer-lasting results can be achieved with old style pure forms of mesmerism-style hypnosis.

The typical treatment session is made up of seven very simple steps:

1. Build a rapport with the client when he or she arrives, and fill out a client questionnaire.

2. Induce the hypnotic trance state.

3. Deepen the hypnotic trance state.

4. Do some ego-strengthening therapy because most issues are due to a lack of willpower, self-confidence, self-image, and/or self-esteem.

5. Do the specific therapy techniques targeted to be effective and totally relevant to whatever the client's particular issue is.

6. Implant the major post-hypnotic suggestion that each time the client listens to the backup audio recording, it is just as effective as if you were there in person.

7. Awaken the client from the trance feeling fantastic.

At stage five, which is the specific therapy, I tend to use my unique approach of Complete Mind Therapy (CMT) because it is proven to be so effective, and it speeds up the treatment process immensely by eliminating the need for using the meta or Milton model's line of questioning.

With NLP, quite literally anything and everything is possible. To use a famous phrase, "What the mind of man can perceive and believe, it can achieve." Yes, these techniques help us to help ourselves and others to believe that they can, will, and have made all the changes to their lives that are necessary for total success and happiness.

Consciously, people look to NLP for some kind of magic wand miracle cure to their problems. On an unconscious level, they want permission to change, leave the past behind, and to feel it is possible to move forward and become the best possible version of themselves.

I use NLP in every area of my life each and every day. In truth, everyone on this planet does without even realizing it, which is where things can go wrong, as they may be programming themselves in negative ways. But, when you are aware of how your personal neck-top computer — more commonly known as your brain — works, it is possible to ensure that all your self-talk and personal suggestions are those of a positive nature. It is also possible to filter out any negative messages that may be thrown at us by the outside world.

NLP is effective in any and all areas of life, as long as you understand that it does have its limitations and is not so much of the Jedi mind control trickery that many have falsely been led to perceive it as.

Essentially, NLP in everyday life, whether business or personal, is about understanding human nature — how we react when on our own, how this differs when we are in groups, how it differs in the workplace, and so on. To that end, I would recommend anyone who wants to become a far better NLPer to study the works of the behaviorists, namely Ivan Pavlov, John Watson, and B. F. Skinner.

NLP is also important for building rapport. The old saying is that people like people who are like them; this tends to imply that if you have similar interests and act in similar manners, you will have rapport together. Though this is true to some extent and has certainly led to the NLP approach of mirroring people's behaviors and matching them to create rapport, it is actually more a case of the fact that people like people who like them.

Hypnotherapy and NLP are one and the same, as I have already explained. Indeed, NLP is nothing more than hypnotherapy with the most effective bits taken out. I do not mean relaxotherapy, like many do today, but pure hypnosis being used to treat people as it was many years ago in its purest form.

Just like anything in life, the more practice you get in the real world, the more automatic it becomes for you to develop an almost laser-like instinct that enables you to target, identify, and solve a client's problem. I do this in the fastest time possible without the need for all the usual questioning and other long-winded procedures that those starting out are often encouraged to use in conventional NLP trainings.

Anchoring is very important because, generally speaking, negative issues affecting us are happening because of a memory or trigger that has been "anchored" into place. By collapsing these anchors, we can leave those triggers behind and move forward with positive changes in our lives. In the same manner, sometimes we need to help clients "anchor" positive things in place to both override negatives from the past and also to give them the resources they need to achieve their desired outcomes.

I have had many successes with NLP and CMT. One of the most unusual was a woman who came to me in the mid-1990s with a morbid fear of traffic wardens, those people who give you tickets and fines for parking in the wrong place. The mere sight of a picture of someone in a traffic warden uniform would bring about cold sweats and trigger a panic attack. I used the Phobia Cure pattern, and within 10 minutes, she was fine and looking at the picture. Next, I cemented these positive changes in place by using my one-session approach of CMT. We then took her out to confront real-life traffic wardens, and she was fine. This treatment and my client's success in overcoming the phobia were featured on the front page and also as a double page spread inside *The Sun*, which is Britain's highest readership national daily newspaper.

If people working with NLP believe they can work on their own using these methods, then they can. However, it is my experience that the vast majority of people prefer to look up at an authority figure, which the therapist is perceived to be. Positive levels of belief and expectancy in the treatment working are enhanced and amplified when an authority figure is in charge of and guiding the process. Many people feel the need to be given permission to change, which is where the therapist offers something that the person often cannot offer themselves.

I would suggest visiting **www.hypnotherapycourse.net** for the best way to learn everything you will need to know to become a truly confident, competent, and qualified advanced master practitioner of NLP, while also becoming a skilled master hypnotherapist. Access the site, and look down the left toolbar for the button that says "Neuro-Linguistic Programming."

NLP is supported by science; it is supported by the same science that shows us how powerful and effective the placebo effect is. The largest element of any successful NLP or hypnotherapy intervention is the correct understanding and use of the true psychology of the placebo effect, which is something that is sadly missing from the vast majority of courses on the market today.

Chapter 9

THE META AND MILTON MODELS

This chapter discusses the meta and Milton models. It will begin with the meta model. NLP co-founders, Bandler and Grinder first wrote about the meta model in their 1975 book *The Structure of Magic: A Book About Language and Therapy, Vol. 1.* An easy way to think about the premise of the meta model is to remember the presupposition, "The map is not the territory." In other words, everyone makes a model or prototype of the world. The prototype or model that people make is not actually the world, but their own representation of the world. You use your mind and words to create a copy or an approximation of the world, but your representations can never be complete or completely accurate. NLP points to three problems with creating wholly accurate representations. These are deletions, distortions, and generalizations, which will be discussed later in the chapter.

There are 13 verbal patterns associated with the meta model. Observing these patterns in your own speech can help you move through limitations, improve communication, and revise mental maps.

Meta Model Processes

You, as well as everyone else, has a mental map. The map cannot accommodate unlimited information so you must develop a shorthand, which results in deletions, distortions, and generalizations. In other words, too much information would overload the mind so you must choose or condense what you can represent. Sometimes these deletions, distortions, and generalizations are useful or benign. In other cases, what you choose to represent can support limiting thoughts or block successful communication.

Deletions, distortions, and generalizations most often fall into a category of one of the 13 verbal patterns that make up the meta model. A discussion of each category, and a list of patterns, follows.

Distortions

You have perceptions that are based on your sensory experiences. Distortion allows you to manipulate, modify, or shift those perceptions. Consider the following examples:

Jane goes down to her kitchen to brew a pot of coffee one morning. As she switches on the light, she sees many ants on the counter. Later, when she calls her pest control provider, she tells the agent there were millions of ants all over her kitchen.

Paul was attacked by robbers, and he was embarrassed and afraid. He thought he might be killed. When the detectives question him, he only says a thief snatched his wallet and ran.

Zachary loves Spiderman. He has seen the movie many times. Each time he wears his costume, he imagines he can swing on webs. When his mother asks him about what he did on the playground, he tells her he swung from a tree and rescued a puppy.

Distortion allows you to describe an experience not necessarily how it happened but the way that it seemed to happen to you. Distortions can take a number of forms. They can be deliberate as in Paul's case, based in fantasy as in Zachary's case, or a way to modify or explain an experience as in Jane's case.

Generalizations

Generalizations are a common shorthand. Consider the following:

Susan asked her mother for permission to go to the fall dance. When her mother says she cannot go, Susan responds, "You *never* let me go anywhere."

Larry and Janet are arguing about money. Janet shouts, "Why are you *always* so wasteful?"

When asked why he will not make a charitable donation to the local homeless shelter, Tom says, "*All* homeless people are lazy drug addicts.

When you generalize, you use a piece of information or a perception you got under one circumstance and apply it to every similar circumstance. In other words, you carry a previous perception into play in a different scenario. In some cases, generalizations can be helpful. Parents use generalization to keep children away from danger. For example, children are warned not to talk to or get into cars with strangers. Because children are not yet old enough to determine when strangers might be safe, they are told to apply the rule to *all* strangers.

Generalizations can also be harmful.

Unpopular at school, Anna believes everyone hates her and no one likes her.

Every time Richard sits down to do his math homework, he thinks, "I am never going to get this right."

Deletions

When you delete, you present restricted or vague information, or you highlight some parts of the experience while ignoring other parts. Consider the following examples:

"I do not think I can handle this situation any longer." This sentence restricts information about the situation that cannot be handled any longer. For example, what is the situation that cannot be handled any longer?

"If I had better clothes I would be more popular." This sentence is vague because it does not establish what constitutes better clothes.

"People do not like me." This sentence provides no information about who the people are.

Tammy was having a great time at the game until someone spilled a drink on her. Later, when her mom asked about the game, she did not mention anything about how close the game was or how exciting it was that her team won during overtime. Tammy only told her mom that someone spilled a drink on her. In this example, Tammy deleted most of the experience and highlighted only the negative part.

Deletions can be especially harmful when they are used to support limiting beliefs. In these cases, deletions are used to highlight examples or proof of the limiting beliefs. Any evidence that contradicts the limiting belief is deleted. For example, Kenny is learning to ride a bike. In the first few minutes of practice, he fell seven times. One time, he stayed on the bike for a few seconds. When Kenny talks about learning to ride a bike, he only mentions that he fell. It is as if he does not even remember that he was successful. Kenny's choice to focus on the negative and delete the positive does not support his stated goal of wanting to learn to ride a bike.

Using the Meta Model

Expressed language is inefficient in its ability to fully capture experience. When you communicate, your words provide only surface information that is only a shadow of the deeper experience. The limits with preventing an accurate picture of the territory result in communication that is filtered through your own unique maps. Those maps determine what and how you distort, generalize, and delete when you communicate.

Understanding meta models can help you communicate better by being mindful of your own deletions, distortions, and generalizations. The meta model can also foster better understanding in communication with others because you recognize the difference between the surface structure of communication and the deep structure of experience. You can ask the kinds of questions required to close the gap between surface and deep structure.

Using the meta model in communication begins simply by listening closely. Consider the following example from an article by the author. As you read, notice any generalizations, distortions, or deletions.

Welcome to Living Simply News

In a rush and hurry world, we often forget the restorative power of slowing down or even being still. I am going to remind and encourage you with Living Simply News.

Slowing can help us quiet our minds. In that quiet space, we can get clear about the things that really matter and let go of those things that do not.

Whether you are now living simply or just wanting to learn more about slowing down and being more deliberate, Living Simply News will include the ideas, inspiration, and information you need.

Think of Living Simply News as your companion on this journey. Let each biweekly newsletter serve as a gentle reminder of the commitment you have made to yourself to do less — buying, scheduling, wasting, moving on autopilot, etc. — and get more — joy, connection, satisfaction, time for what really matters.

There is more than one way, and just as many reasons, to live simply. Many of us go, buy, and do so much that much of what we do and have has lost meaning for us. We have not been able to find the satisfaction we thought having and doing more would bring. Or, perhaps we are satisfied but are concerned about how the way we live impacts our environment. Maybe we just want more time for family, friends, and hobbies. No matter the motivation, Living Simply is here to help.

When you subscribe, you can do so with confidence that you will never receive any spam, and that your privacy will always be respected. Your information will never be sold or shared. In fact, I will only know your name if you choose to share it when you correspond with me via e-mail or the forums.

The decision to live simply is often motivated by our personal values and goals. I hope you will help make the newsletter and site representative of our diverse paths by sharing your own unique perspective of living simply.

Let me hear from you. Do you have an idea for recycling without clutter, teaching children about conservation, or making the transition to TV-free living? I hope you will share it.

Using the meta model with spoken or written communication allows you to intervene with questions to provide clarity. Look at the same article now with highlights on the generalizations, distortions, and deletions.

Welcome to Living Simply News

In a rush and hurry world, we often forget the restorative power of slowing down or even being still. I am going to remind and encourage you with Living Simply News.

Generalization: "In a rush and hurry world we often forget..." assumes all readers are experiencing the world as rushed and hurried and all readers forget the restorative power of slowing down.

Distortion: Describing the world as rushed and hurried is only one of many ways that people, including the article writer, experience the world.

Slowing can help us quiet our minds. In that quiet space, we can get clear about the things that really matter and let go of those things that do not.

Deletion: What are the things that really matter? What things do not matter?

Deletion: Slow(ing) compared to what?

Generalization: "Slowing can help us quiet our minds" assumes that every reader has the problem of a mind that needs slowing and the goal of slowing the mind.

Whether you are now living simply or just wanting to learn more about slowing down and being more deliberate, Living Simply News will include the ideas, inspiration, and information you need.

Deletion: Leaves the reader wondering, "more deliberate than what?"

Generalization: Assumes every reader will need the ideas, inspiration, and information to be offered.

Think of Living Simply News as your companion on this journey. Let each biweekly newsletter serve as a gentle reminder of the commitment you have made to yourself to do less — buying, scheduling, wasting, moving on autopilot, etc. — and get more — joy, connection, satisfaction, time for what really matters.

Deletion: Is not clear about the journey being planned.

Generalization: Assumes each reader has made a personal commitment.

Distortion: Does not include any of a number of other commitments that are possible or could have been made among readers.

There is more than one way, and just as many reasons, to live simply. Many of us go, buy, and do so much that much of what we do and have has lost meaning for us. We have not been able to find the satisfaction we thought having and doing more would bring. Or, perhaps we are satisfied but are concerned about how the way we live impacts our environment. Maybe we just want more time for family, friends, and hobbies. No matter the motivation, Living Simply is here to help.

Deletion: What are the ways to live simply? What is living simply?

Deletion: What satisfaction did you think "having and doing more would bring?"

Deletion: Satisfied compared to what?

When you subscribe, you can do so with confidence that you will never receive any spam, and that your privacy will always be respected. Your information will never be sold or shared. In fact, I will only know your name if you choose to share it when you correspond with me via e-mail or the forums.

Generalization: Assumes every reader will subscribe.

The decision to live simply is often motivated by our personal values and goals. I hope you will help make the newsletter and site representative of our diverse paths by sharing your own unique perspective of living simply.

Deletion: Leaves reader to wonder about "our personal values and goals."

Distortion: Highlighting diverse paths seems to leave no room for the fact that the readers likely also share similar paths.

Let me hear from you. Do you have an idea for recycling without clutter, teaching children about conservation, or making the transition to TV-free living? I hope you will share it.

Deletion: Does not include other possible ideas.

The preceding example shows the importance of using the meta model to improve communication and provide greater clarity. It is important to be mindful of distortions, deletions, and generalizations when speaking and listening. The meta model provides a tool for change in that observation of the patterns can highlight deletions, distortions, and generalizations that are not useful. These same observations can help you use language and ask questions to facilitate better communication. Remember to keep rapport as you question the speaker to gain greater clarity. You want to avoid creating any sense that you are badgering with questions or ready to immediately pounce on what sounds like any distortions, deletions, or generalizations. As you listen, question with gentle and respectful curiosity. When you do question, you get a better idea of what the speaker thinks and feels because you ask rather than fill in the blanks with distortions. You will get a clearer picture when you ask questions about deletions rather than accept the picture as described by the speaker. Also, you will understand how the speaker feels about a particular person, experience, place, or thing when you point out generalizations with the goal of getting a specific perspective.

As mentioned earlier, there are 13 language patterns of the meta model. Understanding these patterns can provide tools for change or support limiting thoughts. The following is a list of each pattern and a brief explanation:

1. **Unspecified nouns:** Create ambiguity for the listener. For example: "Get a clue" does not make clear what kind of clue the listener should get.

2. **Unspecified referential index:** Leaves out information about who is involved. For example: "People are really fed up with politicians" does not specify which people the speaker refers to.

3. **Comparisons:** Implies that a comparison is being made but does not include any basis for comparison. For example: "Even you should understand the gravity of the situation" does not mention who "you" is being compared to in terms of ability to understand.

4. **Unspecified verbs:** Omit a full description of what is happening. For example: "Stop talking like that" does not answer the question, talking like what?

5. **Nominalizations:** Here verbs are expressed as nouns so a process becomes an event or thing. For example: "Women have no appreciation for complex reasoning" can again become a process by inviting the speaker to consider his or her own appreciation of women.

6. **Modal operators of possibility:** Include variations of the words can or could. For example: "I cannot stand this job another day" invites reflection on the possibility of what would happen if the speaker could stand this job another day.

7. **Modal operators of necessity:** Include variations of the words have and must. For example: "I must find a way to get into that club" leaves the listener to wonder what will happen if the speaker is not able to get into that club.

8. **Universal quantifiers:** Use words to generalize without including any point of reference. For example: "You always comb your hair that way" leaves the listener to wonder about any exceptions to the "always" as stated by the listener. The listener may also begin considering times he or she has styled hair in a different way.

9. **Presuppositions:** Omits the underlying message, which is assumed or presupposed to be true for the statement to make sense. For example: "My best friend is pregnant with twins" does not mention the gender of the friend, but gender is assumed by the listener.

10. **Mind reading:** Implies one can know how another person is feeling or what he or is thinking without any meaningful evidence of the assumed feeling, motivation, or thought. For example: "You did that just to make me look ridiculous" might leave the listener wondering how the speaker arrived at that conclusion.

11. **Complex equivalence:** Assume a relationship between two disparate events or ideas. For example: "My co-worker did not smile or say good morning to me today; he must be really angry with me."

12. **Cause and effect:** Assumes that one thing logically follows from another even though there is no proof that the events have any relationship to or impact on one another. For example: "Every time I plan a picnic it rains" may suggest that planning a picnic brings on or causes rain when, in fact, the two events are completely unrelated. Sometimes it rains even when the speaker does not plan a picnic, and sometimes the speaker enjoys a picnic on a sunny, dry day.

13. **Unspecified adjectives:** The speaker is not clear about the meaning of the adjectives being used. For example: "Why do you look so sad" does not make clear or describe what constitutes a sad looking face.

Because of the difficulty in using language to adequately communicate or represent your experiences, some meta model language pattern violations are inevitable. Your job in communicating with yourself — with internal dialogue — and with others is to clarify meaning to present the most accurate and honest representation of facts on the whole.

The Milton Model

Another important NLP model is the Milton model, which is the second and comparatively more vague of the models. This model was created by NLP founders Grinder and Bandler and named for Milton Erickson (1901-1980), a psychiatrist and hypnotherapist. *For more on Milton, see Chapter 1.* The Milton model uses hypnotic language with the goal of deliberately creating distortions, deletions, and generalizations.

With the Milton model, the speaker is deliberately vague, which invites the listener to search his or her own mind to fill in any blanks using his or her own feelings and experiences. Think of the Milton model like a blank, fill-in-the-dot picture. How the listener colors or if the listener colors the picture and connects the dots will vary based on that person's experience. As the listener searches for information to fill in the blanks left by the speaker, he or she enters a trance when leaving the conscious mind to inhabit the unconscious mind. In the unconscious mind, the listener searches for any information that yields individual meaning about the statement or question being considered. For example, consider the statement, "Think of a time when you felt sad." The listener might come up with any number of experiences of being sad. The listener may even briefly re-experience the feeling while searching memories.

Some of the patterns included in the Milton model include tag questions, conversational postulates, and ambiguity. A brief explanation and example of each follows.

Milton model language patterns

Tag questions: Tag questions are added to the end of a statement that invites the listener to answer the question affirmatively. *For more information, see Chapter 2.* This pattern encourages the listener toward a course of action. For example: "Now that rehearsals are completed, you are ready for opening night, are you not?"

Conversational postulates: These are questions that invite the reader to respond with an action rather than the implied yes or no. For example, when someone asks if you can give them a hand, rarely is the expected response a simple yes. Instead, what is expected is some kind of offer of assistance.

Ambiguity: With ambiguity, it can be difficult to arrive at a complete conclusion about what is really happening. For example: "John is traveling" is unclear how John is traveling. Also, the statement leaves the listener to assume the purpose, destination, and duration of John's travels.

Uses of the Milton model

As stated earlier, the Milton model encourages chunking up the content, information, or detail. Doing so allows the listener to search him or herself to assign meaning to the information being discussed. The Milton model uses language patterns that make it easier to access the unconscious mind. Some of the uses for the Milton model include encouraging a more relaxed or trance state, encouraging a course of action, and moving to higher levels of thinking.

The following lists some of the language patterns discussed with the meta model with a brief discussion of how they are used with the Milton model:

Deletions: "Think of a chair." Simply saying this does not give the listener much detailed information. In fact, all the details are deleted, leaving the listener free to assign his or her own unique meaning to the chair.

Cause and effect: "Taking a deep breath makes you feel relaxed." Establishing a causal relationship between these two actions, taking a deep breath and feeling relaxed, provides a suggestion. The suggestion encourages the desired behavior, feeling relaxed, in the listener.

Mind reading: "I know you are wondering." With mind reading, a statement such as this functions like a suggestion. With that suggestion, the listener actually does begin to wonder.

The Milton model is often thought of as the opposite of the meta model. In the simplest terms, the meta model moves toward the specific with language and the Milton model moves away from the specific with language. Many practitioners use both models, often interchangeably.

Chapter 10

NLP PATTERNS

N LP has dozens of patterns. What makes the number of patterns so important is the likelihood that there will be one to help you change or create any desired circumstance in your life. You can use patterns for virtually everything from weight loss to building success in sales and education.

Patterns are Directions for Creating Effective Experiences

How often has someone wondered aloud about a blueprint for life? In essence, that is what a pattern is, a blueprint for creating the life you want. You can use patterns to reprogram behavior and change attitudes or even to get motivated and improve communications. It is not possible to learn every pattern, but learning even a few patterns well can be immensely helpful.

Presentation of Several Basic Patterns

Some of the patterns of NLP have been mentioned previously in this book. These include the Godiva Chocolate pattern and the Swish pattern. Because NLP has so many more patterns than can be covered in this book, the book will highlight only five. A brief explanation of each follows. An exercise is included with our first pattern, the Autobiography pattern.

The Autobiography pattern

You, like everyone else, have a story about who you are, what your experiences have been, what you can do, and so forth. The Autobiography pattern is a great exercise to use for reflection and appreciation of the whole of who you are; it allows you to move your gaze for the trees of your life to the forest. What often happens when you think of yourself is you lose sight of the big picture because you are focused on the small things like why you are having trouble in a particular area or wishing you could be different in another area. The Autobiography pattern invites you to look at yourself in much the same way that you would regard someone you love.

Think of a loved one, such as a child, spouse, parent, partner, grandparent, or friend. How you respond to that person when he or she makes a mistake is likely much more patient and loving than the way you would respond to yourself in the same circumstance. The Autobiography pattern can help you learn to have as much appreciation and patience for yourself as you would have for someone you love and someone you love has for you.

EXERCISE 12: APPRECIATING YOURSELF MORE WITH THE AUTOBIOGRAPHY PATTERN

Step 1: To do the Autobiography pattern, begin by finding a quiet place where you will not be interrupted. Spend several minutes allowing yourself to slip into a state of relaxation. You may want to sit in your favorite chair and breathe deeply or begin with a short meditation. As you begin this process, you do not want to feel any tension in your body.

Step 2: As you begin to feel yourself relax, let your mind settle on someone who loves you. Choose someone who knows you well and loves you in spite of your real and imagined faults.

Step 3: With this loving person in mind, see yourself writing your autobiography. Your words and thoughts may be warmed by the thought of the person and the love he or she has for you.

Step 4: Imagine your loved one being right there with you as you move through this process. As you see him or her, be clear about the details. What does he or she look like? See a loving smile; imagine how you feel when you are with him or her.

Step 5: Think about the relationship you have shared and how it has felt to you. Imagine exactly what this person might say when describing his or her feelings for you. Adopt the second perceptual position now. Step into this person's thoughts and feel what he or she feels for you.

Step 6: Write about the experience of seeing yourself through your loved one's eyes. Include what it felt like to feel his or her love for you from that point of view.

Step 7: Sit for several moments reflecting on the feelings you experienced, and notice if there are any changes in what you see in yourself or how you feel about yourself.

Additional Patterns

The Phobia Cure pattern

Many people experience phobias. Phobias are often irrational fears that can range from inconvenient to debilitating. Regardless of the kind of phobia, one strategy for releasing it is the Phobia Cure pattern.

Begin by anchoring a resource state. Obviously, you will want to choose a state that finds you calm and relaxed.

Next, you want to imagine the experience of the phobia as a movie. See the movie from the third perceptual position — the position of the observer. Watching the experience as an observer can help you feel safe because you witness rather than actually take part in the experience. From the third position, see a picture of you having the difficult experience the very first time. For example, if you have a fear of dogs, you may picture yourself standing near the dog before it bit you or chased you. See the movie in black and white. Watch the movie run in reverse, and at the end, let the last image you see fade to black. Now, begin the movie again, this time running in forward. As with the last viewing, let the last image you see fade to black.

You are now ready to run the movie from the first position. Repeat the same process of running the movie backward and forward; remember to let the last image fade to black. After you have done this several times, you are likely to find the phobia is no longer triggered or present.

The As-if pattern

This book has frequently mentioned the presupposition that people have all the resources they need. The As-if pattern helps to marshal those resources needed to move beyond a limiting belief if it is blocking access to a desired outcome. Consider the following example. Jane says to her Spanish instructor, "I will never be able to learn to conjugate verbs." Her teacher might respond by saying, "I wonder if someone were to learn how to conjugate verbs how she or he would do it?" The question helps Jane move beyond the place where she feels stuck to consider the question without the limits she has placed on herself. Jane thinks of the question as if learning how to conjugate verbs is not a problem and as if such learning is possible. Use the same line of question for problems you are trying to work through in your own life.

The Forgiveness pattern

Developed by Connirae and Steve Andreas, the Forgiveness pattern can help to eliminate even old feelings of anger and resentment. Completing this pattern does not mean you excuse the behavior that led to the anger. It does mean that you create some peace for yourself by releasing the negative feelings.

Begin by thinking about the person or thing you feel angry about. Notice how you remember the event. How do you describe it to yourself? Which submodalities do you use? Do you see the event happening? Do you hear it? Do you feel it?

Now recall a time when you felt angry but were able to find forgiveness after the event. How would you describe this experience? In what way is your ability to recall the event different and similar?

Switch submodalities. If you felt the anger you are still experiencing in your stomach, experience it now visually as you did when you were able to forgive.

Visual Squash pattern

This pattern works to help you develop a new way of thinking about a problem or a conflict. Begin by choosing an image to represent each side of the conflict. A common television example of this practice is the angel on one shoulder and a demon on the other shoulder. In this instance, each visual image is in one of your hands.

Suppose the angel wants to skip cake for dessert and reach for a piece of fruit. The devil, of course, has a different idea — skip the fruit and grab the dessert. The Visual Squash pattern allows you to work out a compromise between the opposing sides. In this example, the angel may decide that it is all right to have cake, just a smaller portion because it would be a nice way to help your friend celebrate his or her birthday. The devil may chime in with a compromise on the fruit agreeing that it will provide longer-term energy for the party you want to attend later in the evening. As each side finds some agreement with the compromise, bring your hands together to merge the two images.

NLP patterns are useful in a variety of practical settings as illustrated by the following examples.

NLP patterns in sales

Some of the most useful NLP patterns for sales involve language and communication patterns. This book has previously discussed the language patterns associated with the Milton and meta models. These models, along with other patterns and strategies like mirroring, anchoring, and matching, help build personal confidence and charisma, both of which are useful in creating rapport.

NLP in education

Chapter 2 discussed the value of the Godiva Chocolate pattern in building motivation to complete a dreaded task. You will recall that the Godiva Chocolate pattern starts with creating an image of something you desire. Use your knowledge about submodalities to make the image as inviting as possible. Next, see yourself doing the task that you have not wanted to do.

Place the image of the thing you desire behind the picture of yourself completing the task you want to get excited about. Imagine a small hole opening in the first picture so you can get a look at the second picture. Notice how good you feel when you get a peek at the second picture. Allow the small hole to close slowly while you hold on to the good feelings. Do this several times until you begin to connect the good feelings with the task you want to do.

NLP for personal change

Chapter 8 discussed the Swish pattern. The Swish pattern switches visual internal representations to create additional options or change behavior. NLP patterns are also useful for changing limiting thoughts and eliminating phobias and fears.

NLP patterns provide a guidebook of ideas for creating the life you want. Each of these patterns helps you access your personal resources to achieve excellence in any arena of your life. It is not necessary to memorize the patterns or familiarize yourself with every pattern. It is enough to understand that you do not have to remain in non-useful states. For every problem that exists, there is a pattern that can help you organize your resources for a solution that works well for your situation.

Conclusion

N LP is an important tool for achieving excellence in your own life. Use NLP to break through limiting beliefs, eliminate phobias, achieve desired outcomes, and operate from your most useful state. There are no limits to what you can do with NLP when you practice and apply the patterns and strategies.

There is much to learn with NLP, or neuro-linguistic programming. The most important things to remember about these revolutionary strategies, presuppositions, and patterns are:

- **If a thing has been done, it can be done.**
  Remember that, at its core, NLP is about modeling human excellence. If you struggle with anything at all, from meeting a sales goal to finishing a marathon or conquering public speaking, know that you can end the struggle by understanding how

someone who was successful with your problem found that success. If someone is experiencing more success that you are with anything, it is probably because he or she brings different resources to the task or uses the same resources differently. Even if you do not feel like you have immediate access to the required resources, remember that you do. People have all the resources they need.

- **You always have immediate access to your desired state.** Remember the power of anchoring to shift a non-useful state to a useful one. If you did not do so *(in Chapter 7)*, take a few moments now to identify your most troubling emotional state. *Use the exercise in that chapter to develop an anchor that can immediately take you back to a more resourceful place.*

- **You can change your mind and your behavior with NLP.** It does not matter how long you have had a behavior or a thought. You can create new thoughts, feelings, and behaviors with NLP.

The following are some of the key ideas from the book. Refer to these often as you work to change your mind and your behavior.

NLP in Sales

When it comes to sales, the keywords are rapport and well-formed outcomes. Using well-formed outcomes can mean

the difference between wishing you could be successful and actually enjoying success. *Review Chapter 4 for
a more detailed discussion.* A quick review of well-formed
outcomes follows.

Transforming goals into well-formed outcomes

Transforming goals into well-formed outcomes can happen
with planning and a few simple steps. Use each of the following steps to improve your outcomes:

- **The goal must be stated in positive terms.** In
  other words, the goal should identify what you
  want or value. According to Dr. Norman Vincent
  Peale, author of *The Power of Positive Thinking*,
  positive thinking leads to confidence, success, and
  achievement. Peale, a Protestant preacher who died
  in 1993 at the age of 95, is widely acknowledged
  as founder of the practice and idea of positive
  thinking. Positive thinking is strongly supported
  in NLP.

- **The goal must be sensory based.** A sensory-based
  goal connects you to the outcome by allowing you to
  use your senses to describe how it feels to achieve
  what you want. Using your senses to experience
  your goal engages your subconscious mind in
  support of the outcome. When your subconscious
  mind embraces the outcome, feelings of resistance,
  and the resulting self-sabotage, are greatly reduced
  or eliminated.

- **The goal must be one that you value and can control.** Your interest in achieving the goal must come from your unique personal motivation or mission. Your personal mission speaks to larger life questions, such as who you are or want to be in relation to the world, what you think your purpose is in life, and how you plan to honor that purpose.

- **The goal should have a context.** You can contextualize your goal by asking questions that clarify the circumstances of the outcome. Providing context for your goal is much like giving the goal an anchor in reality.

- **The goal should fit your individual values, needs, and interests.** Your goals are as personal as your shoes. Your motivation, resources, approach, rewards, and obstacles are uniquely yours. Additionally, the goal should not be at odds with the values, needs, and interests of the systems — i.e. family, faith community, work environment — around you. You, along with everyone else, are part of a larger community. Your actions impact the people around you. When your actions adversely impact the systems you are a part of, the resulting feelings may cause you to abandon your goals.

NLP for Successful Communication

Read Chapter 3 for a more detailed discussion of the four pillars, including rapport, of NLP. These pillars form the ba-

sis for the NLP philosophy, and these pillars support all NLP concepts.

Behavioral flexibility

As the word flexibility suggests, this pillar is concerned with one's ability to adapt his or her actions as a strategy for influencing a particular response from and in response to another person.

Sensory acuity

Paying attention to small changes in facial expression or eye movement helps you determine if what you are saying resonates with or annoys others. It is important to note here that body language is as unique as individuals themselves.

Rapport

The goal in creating rapport is not wholesale agreement of everything that is being communicated but rather to show the other person that you understand what they are trying to communicate.

There are three output channels: words, voice, and body. To get a full understanding of what is being communicated, you must survey, interpret, and respond to all three output channels.

Outcome thinking

Outcome thinking encourages you to clearly define what you want so you are more likely to get it. Outcome thinking helps you shift from the problem to the process of considering solutions.

The four pillars of NLP form the building blocks for successful communication.

NLP in Education

NLP offers a number of uses for educators. Teachers who understand the representational systems can target their lessons for maximum impact. For example, teachers can target their instruction to be particularly appealing to students who are visual, kinesthetic, or auditory learners. *Review Chapter 2 for a discussion of representational systems in the classroom, as well as the teacher's tool box.* The following is a brief overview.

Six NLP strategies for the teacher's tool box

Teaching can be a challenge and a joy. Find more joy in the teaching experience with the following tools that are helpful for teachers, as well as students:

- **Use language to improve learning.** Understand the importance of language and how individual students will take meaning from what is and is not said.

- **Achieve agreement in the classroom.** It is a good idea for teachers to present choices so that whichever choice the student makes, the desired outcome is achieved.

- **Speak with positive assumptions.** Teachers can use positive assumptions to encourage children.

- **Cover your bases.** Foster feelings of inclusion with the NLP strategy of covering all bases.

- **Use yes tags to get agreement.** Using yes tags is another strategy teachers can use to gain agreement or cooperation from students.

- **Use positive language to improve outcomes.** Use language to help students focus on desired behavior.

NLP for Personal Change

One of the most useful tools NLP has to offer with creating change is anchors. You will recall that anchors associate an internal response with an external stimulus. *A discussion of anchors is included in Chapter 7.*

There are three important points to remember about anchors, which are:

- The anchor should be set right at or just a few seconds before the most intense or peak portion of the recall experience.

- The anchor should be unique. Avoid an anchor that you commonly use.

- Finally, your anchor should be consistent so it is firmly and reliably established.

NLP for Understanding Motivation

Use metaprograms to understand motivation in yourself and others. *An explanation of this is included in Chapter 6.* There are seven common programs that most people employ to some degree:

- **Toward versus away from:** Toward versus away from describes a common motivation strategy or metaprogram. As you will recall, individuals motivated in a "toward" direction take action in anticipation of a reward. Individuals motivated in an "away from" direction take action to avoid a negative consequence.

- **Proactive versus reactive:** Proactive people are more likely to jump in first and consider later; these kinds of people are initiators. Reactive people are responders; they consider what is happening before jumping in.

- **Sameness versus difference:** In this category, people are motivated by creating change or difference or maintaining things as they are. People with a sameness metaprogram value constancy.

- **Internal versus external:** People with an internal motivation filter ideas, values, and standards through their own individual standards. As you might expect, people with external motivation derive their feedback from external sources.

- **Options versus procedures:** The difference here is between actively seeking options and acting by the book. The short definition of this program might sound like the difference between possibility and process.

- **Global versus detail:** Like the word suggests, people who operate from global metaprograms prefer the big picture. These kinds of people look for the overall view and work from there, believing the details can be filled in once the general overview has been established. The opposite kind of metaprogram, detail, is motivated by smaller bits of information.

- **Introvert versus extrovert:** The terms have a slightly different connotation with NLP where the focus is not on the difference between having a shy or outgoing personality. Instead, the focus is on how your metaprogram leads you to restore your emotional energy. People who operate from an introvert metaprogram feel restored by alone time. Extroverts find their energy in the company of others.

Presuppositions

Finally, the presuppositions are worth memorizing and are repeated here for your convenience.

The map is not the territory

In NLP, the map is like a software program that governs what you think, say, and do. As in the world of technology, software programs vary widely. The map can only be a partial representation of the actual possible territory, which is vast. In other words, one person's map can never fully express what is. The map can only express information that has been filtered through an individual's perceptions.

People respond based on their individual map

You, like everyone else, have your own individual map for the world. This map is drawn as you collect information through your senses — visual (sight), auditory (hearing), kinesthetic (feeling), olfactory (smelling), and gustatory (tasting) — and interpret it based on your own values, beliefs, and background. Much of that information settles in your subconscious mind without your conscious awareness. You use information from your conscious and subconscious minds to form beliefs, feelings, and values. This information also governs your actions.

There is no failure — only feedback

Language matters not just when you talk to others but when you talk to yourself, too. When you attempt to do something and find that your results do not match your anticipated outcome, it is most useful to view the experience as one you can learn from rather than one that was wasted or failed. If you choose to regard the experience in this way, you will look for information you can use in reworking your anticipated outcome, such as lining up originally overlooked resources, making a secondary plan for navigating obstacles, or planning how you will talk yourself through moments of fear, doubt, and hesitation.

The meaning of communication is the response it gets

This presupposition is especially useful for parents of teenagers. Parents intend to communicate love and concern. What teens often hear is angry, frustrated badgering, and of course, they respond in kind. The original message — such as, "I care about what happens to you, and I want you to be safe" — is lost amidst hurt and angry feelings, and in extreme cases, the relationship begins to suffer.

If what you are doing is not working, do something different

This concept seems simple enough when you read it, but is it really? Being honest, most people can find multiple examples of things they do that they know do not work. Do any of these sound familiar? You wait until the last minute to buy or send birthday cards so they always arrive late; you put off that paper or presentation until the last minute and then get it done but know you could have done better;

you spend outside of your budget; you confide in people who are not trustworthy; or you race around with the kids before school so everyone starts the day feeling cranky and frazzled. The examples of how people all continue to do things that do not work are endless.

You cannot not communicate

Communication is more than what you say; it is both verbal *and* nonverbal. Everything about you, from your clothes to your body language, communicates a message. For example, how might you express interest in what a person says without verbalizing your interest? How can you tell if someone is worried, confident, happy, or angry? People use language, facial expressions, and body cues that reveal something about the way they think and feel. They express themselves many different ways, including through their choice of words and style of dress.

Individuals have all the resources they need to achieve their desired outcomes

Everyone has the power to create change in his or her own life. An expression says, "Even a broken clock is right twice each day." Applied to individuals, the expression could be interpreted to mean that everyone, no matter the circumstance, has a strong and perfect place from which to build. Accepting the idea that individuals have all the resources they need requires one to search for those resources in themselves and others, no matter how deeply they are hidden. This presupposition allows you to change your interpretation of some behaviors and reconsider others. For example, suppose you have tried to lose weight in the past without success. The problem is not the goal or your ability to accomplish it; it is your willingness to understand how to direct your internal resources toward accomplishing the goal.

Underlying every behavior is a positive intent

The presupposition that underlying every behavior is a positive intent is not a license to commit or reason to condone bad behavior. Examples of bad behavior include bullying, hitting, yelling, stealing, and lying. Consider the legendary English hero Robin Hood who is said to have robbed from the rich — negative behavior — to give to the poor — positive intent. When you uncover the underlying positive intention behind bad behavior — wanting to belong or feel included, wanting to be heard, or warding off danger or hunger, for example — you can look for and adopt new behaviors to support the intention. In your own life, this would mean looking for the reward or payoff you get for bad behavior. You must then look for positive ways to get the same or a better payoff so your behavior change is supported. This presupposition invites you to have more compassion for others and yourself by making it possible to separate the deed from the doer. This presupposition also helps you understand behavior and develop appropriate motivation for changing behavior you no longer want.

People are much more than their behavior

You probably have heard about separating the deed from the doer. Individuals are quite complex and cannot be fully understood just by what they do. Sometimes, behaviors are contradictory or happen only in limited or extreme circumstances. Think of a religious leader who has profoundly touched hundreds of lives but has also misappropriated hundreds of dollars. Some behavior represents only a glimmer of what is really possible. Think of a student with above average intelligence who consistently underperforms. You are more than what you do because the possibilities for what you can do are limitless. Behavior is or can be always changing. It is not fixed. Understanding that people are much more than their behavior helps you know you are not limited by what you have done. The ability to remove limits by doing something different or better is always available to you.

People make the best choices available to them

You may wonder how people end up in jail, on jobs they hate, or with addictions. Everyone makes choices based on his or her own individual history, values, beliefs, and experiences. People do the best they can with what they believe is available to them. You bring your own unique worldview and perception to each decision you make. In some cases, your worldview obscures the full range of possibilities, leaving you to select from limited choices. When you remember that the map is not the territory, you understand you can broaden your worldview or rework your maps to add more choices. Remember that even when you do not see a choice, there likely is one there that will become visible with a different map or a different perspective. You have probably experienced this when you explained a problem to a friend who offered you a perspective or solution that never even occurred to you.

If you take nothing else from this book, keep the presuppositions with you always. They are your guide to thinking in a consistently resourceful way, which will ultimately lead you where you want to go.

NLP is growing in popularity in motivational circles

From its very humble beginnings in the 1970s, NLP has grown into an international phenomena. Many of the practices and ideas have found acceptance among mainstream therapists and counselors. Thousands of books have been written on the various aspects of NLP. These are complemented by hundreds of workshops and trainings and even more visual media, such as videos and DVDs.

Many of the ideas born out of the work of NLP founders Grinder and Bandler have also found their way into advertising, marketing, sales, and corporate trainings. NLPs popularity is due in no small measure to the success it has helped so many people experience. Problems and beliefs that seemed so deeply entrenched that they could not be moved have been dissolved with one or two treatments.

The ultimate value of NLP is the value it helps you discover within.

Use the techniques to improve both professional and personal lives

NLP is equally useful in professional and personal settings. Any setting that includes people in communication with themselves and or the people around them can benefit from NLP. Among the most useful ways that NLP impacts personal and professional settings is its ability to build rapport. Poor communication is among the biggest problems facing people regardless of the setting. NLP offers the tools to create better, more meaningful understanding and connection.

This book has been a brief introduction to some of the ideas of NLP. The field is quite broad, and there is a lot of good information available. As you continue your studies, consider reading from some of the following references.

References for Further Study

1. *Get the Life You Want: The Secrets to Quick and Lasting Change with Neuro-Linguistic Programming.* Richard Bandler

2. *Awaken the Giant Within: How to take Control of Your Mental, Emotional, Physical and Financial Destiny!* Anthony Robbins

3. *Unlimited Power: The New Science of Personal Achievement.* Anthony Robbins

4. *Frogs into Princes.* Richard Bandler and John Grinder

5. *Using Your Brain – for a Change.* Richard Bandler

6. *The 7 Habits of Highly Effective People.* Steven R. Covey

7. *The Structure of Magic, Vol. 2: A Book about Communication and Change.* Grinder and Bandler

8. *Aligning Perceptual Positions.* Connirae Andreas

9. *Heart of the Mind: Engaging your Inner Power to Change with Neuro-Linguistic Programming.* Connirae and Steven Andreas

10. *Values Based Leadership.* Kelly Patrick Gerling and Charles Sheppard

Glossary

Anchoring: Connects an internal response with an external trigger. Anchors can be visual, auditory, kinesthetic, olfactory, or gustatory.

Associated: Having a remembered experience from the first person perceptual position. In connecting with the experience though your own sense modes, you see, hear, and feel what is happening while it happens.

Auditory: Concerned with hearing; one of the sense modes.

Away from: A type of metaprogram where the preference of the person is to move away from a punishment. The opposite of the away from motivation is a toward motivation.

Break state: Interruption of your current emotional state.

Chunking: Gathering pieces of information into smaller or larger groups or pieces. Chunking up organizes pieces of information into larger groups, while chunking down moves information into smaller groups.

Congruence: Finding agreement among all of the internal behaviors, thoughts, feelings, and beliefs.

Deep structure: The inherent or implied, but unexpressed, meaning in language.

Deletion: Expressed language that does not include deep structure. In other words, the details have not been included, leaving the listener to make assumptions about what has been said.

Dissociated: Having a remembered experience from the third person perceptual position. In other words, not connecting with the experience, but seeing it as an observer.

Distortion: Using language to present an inaccurate picture or description of an event.

Ecology: The larger system in which individuals function. NLP advocates looking at the entire life — for example, work, place of faith, family, friends — to see if changes can be supported or if they will be undermined by unintended consequences or outcomes.

Elicitation: Involves using questions to understand internal processing.

Eye accessing cues: Eye movement patterns that reveal how a person is processing information or what they are thinking and feeling.

Generalization: Extending a unique or specific experience into a model for every similar group of experiences.

Gustatory: Concerned with taste; one of the sense modes.

Internal representation: Individuals patterns of storing memories, thoughts, and ideas and experiences using each of the sense modes.

Kinesthetic: Concerned with feeling — both tactile and emotional; one of the sense modes.

Matching: Copying the behavior patterns of another person for the purpose of creating rapport.

Meta model: One of the first two models developed by NLP co-founders Grinder and Bandler, meta models gather information into smaller chunks to improve communication by removing generalizations, distortions, and deletions.

Milton model: Named for noted hypnotherapist Milton Erikson, this model chunks up details, allowing the listener to access the subconscious in search of information.

Mirroring: Adopting some of the behavior patterns of another person for the purpose of building rapport.

Modeling: Copying the successful behavior of others to achieve success in your own life.

Olfactory: Concerned with smelling; one of the sense modes.

Pacing: Establishing rapport with matching some of the behaviors, such as voice tone. Pacing ends with leading. Here is an example of the pattern: pace, pace, pace, lead.

Perceptual position: One of the points of view from which to regard a situation. The positions are first (yourself), second (the listener), and third (an observer).

Predicates: Words that reveal which representational system the speaker uses. For example, "I see" would suggest a visual representational system.

Presupposition: A statement with an underlying meaning that is assumed to be true.

Rapport: The process of building meaningful connection with another person.

Representational systems: Related to the sense modes that are used to represent experiences, memories, and ideas internally.

Resources: A broad term used to include all the things used to achieve a desired outcome. Examples of resources include beliefs, language, and emotional states.

State: How a person is thinking and feeling at a given moment.

Submodalities: Distinctions that allow for fine tuning the sense modes. For example, in the visual submodality, there is the ability to brighten, darken, or remove color from an internal representation.

Visual: Concerned with sight; one of the sense modes.

Well-formed outcome: The formula for achieving a desired outcome, which says it must be stated in the positive, self-controlled, right sized, and ecological.

Bibliography

Andreas, Steve, and Faulkner, Charles, eds. *NLP: The New Technology of Achievement*. New York: Harper Collins, 1994.

Beever, Sue. *Happy Kids, Happy You: Using NLP to Bring Out the Best in Ourselves and the Children We Care for*. Wales: Crown House Publishing, 2009.

Culbert, Samuel, and Rout, Lawrence. *Get Rid of the Performance Review!: How Companies Can Stop Intimidating and Start Managing*. New York: Business Plus, 2010.

Galatiltyte, Rasa. *Beyond Rapid Therapy: Modern NLP Concepts & Methods*. Inner Patch Publishing, 2009.

Terry, Roger, and Churches, Richard. *NLP for Teacher: How to Be a Highly Effective Teacher.* Wales: Crown House Publishing, 2008.

Terry, Roger, and Churches, Richard. *The NLP Toolkit for Teachers, Trainers and School Leaders.* Wales: Crown House Publishing, 2009.

Vaknin, Shlomo. *NLP for Beginners: Only the Essentials.* Inner Patch Publishing, 2009.

Author Biography

Barbara P. Gibson works as safehouse director for a non-profit agency serving survivors of domestic violence. Also a freelance writer, Gibson has found NLP principles and practices to be useful in her personal and professional life. She lives in Decatur, Georgia, just outside of Atlanta.

Index

A

Alfred Korzybski, 34

Anchor, 26, 40, 92, 103, 111, 142, 144, 147, 159, 162-163, 181-186, 188, 190-204, 227, 258, 260, 263-264

Anchoring, 26, 52, 123-124, 149, 163, 179, 181, 183, 191-194, 197, 227, 250, 253, 258, 275

Anxiety, 55, 110, 112, 118, 184-185, 193-194, 200, 202

As-if pattern, 251

Auditory, 36, 70, 79-81, 93-94, 122, 151-152, 156-157, 162-163, 191-192, 199, 203, 205-206, 211, 262, 266, 275

Autobiography pattern, 248-249

B

Behavioral flexibility, 24, 90, 92, 129-130, 261

Break state, 25, 92, 101, 192, 195-197, 275

C

Chunking, 245, 276

Circle of Excellence pattern, 25, 121-122

Conscious competence, 28-29, 135, 176

Conscious incompetence, 28, 30, 135, 175

Cue, 23, 131

E

Education, 50, 89, 123, 247, 254, 262

Elicitation, 276

EMDR, 64

Extrovert, 172, 265

Eye movement, 64, 130, 157, 261, 277

Eye movement desensitization and reprocessing, 64

F

Forgiveness pattern, 252

Framing, 24

Frederick Perls, 30

Future pacing, 181-182, 187, 198-200, 204

G

Gestalt therapy, 31

Gregory Bateson, 31, 105

Gustatory, 24, 36, 79, 162, 191-192, 205, 266, 275, 277

H

Hypnosis, 33, 51-52, 176-180, 224-225, 227

I

Introvert, 172, 265

J

John Grinder, 30, 273

K

Kinesthetic, 36, 71, 79, 81, 94, 122, 151-152, 162-163, 191-192, 201, 205-206, 211-212, 262, 266, 275, 277

L

Laura Perls, 30-31

Limiting beliefs, 167, 233, 257

Listener, 34, 40, 69, 71-72, 74, 76, 78, 83-84, 90, 97, 133-135, 150-151, 240-246, 276-278

M

Matching, 52, 70, 82-83, 87, 109, 133-134, 157, 178, 200, 226, 253, 277-278

Meta model, 52, 124, 149, 162, 179, 225, 229-230, 234-

236, 239-240, 243, 245-246, 277

Metaprogram, 25, 165-166, 170-175, 264-265, 275

Milton Erickson, 31, 33-34, 105, 243

Milton model, 34, 50-53, 124, 149, 162, 178, 225, 243-246, 277

Mirroring, 52, 82, 109, 133, 178, 226, 253, 277

N

Negotiation, 78-79, 162

O

Olfactory, 24, 36, 79, 162-163, 191-192, 205, 266, 275, 278

Outcome frame, 137-138

Outcome thinking, 24, 88, 92, 129, 134, 261

P

Pacing, 52, 83-87, 96, 126, 134, 181-182, 187, 198-200, 204, 278

Parent, 103, 113, 184-185, 248

Parenting, 114, 188, 203

Perceptual position, 83, 86, 103, 133, 160, 250, 275-276, 278

Phobia, 65, 123, 227, 249-251

Phobia Cure pattern, 123, 227, 249-250

Pillar, 129, 261

Predicates, 134, 155-157, 278

Presupposition, 34, 40, 44, 58-59, 78, 87, 89, 131, 144, 160, 194, 217, 223, 229, 251, 267-269, 278

Primary representational system, 70, 79-80, 82, 156, 200-201

Productivity, 29, 73, 76, 84-85, 174

PRS, 70, 79-81, 93, 156, 159

R

RACE method, 188-190

Rapport, 20, 24-25, 28-30, 49-50, 52-53, 69-76, 78-80, 82-83, 87, 90, 92-94, 109, 111, 122-123, 126, 129-131, 133-136, 148, 157, 159-160, 162, 164, 169, 177-179, 200, 202, 225-226, 239, 253, 258, 260-261, 272, 277-278

Reframing, 50, 52, 97, 102, 104, 175, 179

Relationship, 40, 47, 75, 94, 108, 149, 160, 163, 168, 177, 242, 245, 250, 267

Reprocessing, 64-65

Richard Bandler, 30-31, 176, 178, 272-273

Robert Dilts, 104-105, 173

S

Sales, 71, 158, 177, 247, 253, 257-258, 271

Self-image, 120, 213, 225

Sensory acuity, 129-130, 178, 261

Speaker, 37, 48, 58, 68, 70, 74, 83-84, 119, 132, 135, 156, 239-244, 278

Squash pattern, 252-253

State, 20, 24-26, 34, 37, 40, 52-53, 62, 64, 73, 91-92, 101, 103, 108-109, 111, 113, 118, 121-122, 139, 144, 146, 159, 167-168, 177-178, 181-185, 187-188, 190-193, 195-204, 208, 213, 215, 218, 225, 245, 249-250, 257-258, 275, 278

Student, 45, 50, 57, 90-91, 94-100, 103, 149, 262-263, 270

Subconscious competence, 28-30, 135, 176

Subconscious incompetence, 28-29, 135, 175

Submodalities, 179, 191, 205, 210-212, 222, 252, 254, 279

Swish pattern, 85-86, 144, 179, 213-215, 220-223, 248, 254

T

Teacher, 281, 50, 94-95, 98-99, 106-108, 123, 184, 251, 262

TOTE model, 201

Trigger, 92, 111, 159, 183, 187, 195-197, 202, 216, 227, 275, 26

V

VAK, 24

Virginia Satir, 31-32

Visual, 32, 36, 70, 79-80, 93, 122, 137, 151-152, 156, 162-163, 165, 191-192, 199, 203, 205-206, 210, 219-220, 223, 252-254, 262, 266, 271, 275, 278-279